How to Write Erotic Fiction and Sex Scenes

Ashley Lister

howtobooks

Published by How To Books Ltd,
Spring Hill House, Spring Hill Road,
Begbroke, Oxford OX5 1RX
Tel: (01865) 375794. Fax: (01865) 379162
info@howtobooks.co.uk
www.howtobooks.co.uk

How To Books greatly reduce the carbon footprint of their books by sourcing
their typesetting and printing in the UK.

First published 2013

British Library Cataloguing in Publication Data
A catalogue record for this book is available from the British Library

ISBN: 978 1 84528 505 0

Produced for How To Books by Deer Park Productions, Tavistock
Typeset by TW Typesetting, Plymouth, Devon
Printed and bound in Great Britain by Bell & Bain Ltd, Glasgow

Contents

Acknowledgements

I'm indebted to all the writers who've given permission for their work to be included in this book. I'm equally indebted to the publishing houses who've given permissions and to all the friends and colleagues who've helped me track down lost friends and favourite authors so that I could make this book as complete as possible.

I also owe a huge debt of gratitude to the friends and family who helped me get this MS to completion. You know who you are. Thank you for being so supportive.

Preface

Of all the literary genres, erotica is the one that can make the strongest physical impression on a reader. Erotica is also the genre that can provoke the strongest critical reactions of condemnation and praise, even from those who've never read the work they're discussing.

- In other words: no other genre compares to erotica.
- We might read horror to enjoy being scared.
- We might read murder mysteries to pit our own wits against a genius detective.
- We might read literary titles to savour the timeless pleasure of a classic.

But no other genre compares to the sexually charged thrill of reading well-written erotica.

There are reasons for this.

Most importantly, erotic fiction is arousing. Because of its taboo associations, erotica remains one of the most compelling genres in all of fiction. As children we used to look up the rude words in the dictionary before exploring anything else in those pages. We went on to giggle at the sex references in supposedly serious works such as the Bible and Shakespeare. Since then many of us have moved on to enjoy reading more explicit fiction. If you're reading this book, the chances are you're now interested in writing explicit fiction.

There are various definitions of erotica. The one I'm most inclined to accept is:

Written literature or art intended to cause sexual arousal.

Admittedly, this definition leaves a broad scope of interpretation. What one person classes as erotica, another person might dismiss as pornography. My own opinion is: if the reader considers the work to be erotic, then it's erotic. It doesn't matter what label anyone else places on the piece.

In the following pages I've included examples of erotic fiction and sex scenes from a host of writers who exemplify good practice in the genre. Because of restrictions of space I've had to overlook many other writers who are equally talented. But I'm happy that the writers in these pages represent some of the best authors currently populating the erotic fiction shelves.

To make the best use of this book you'll need a notepad and pen and the desire to write erotic fiction. There are exercises in most chapters as well as materials to prompt creativity and guidance about the preferred practices within the genre.

The purpose of this book is to show how erotica is currently being written and give some inspiration for those who are interested in writing erotica. Hopefully, by the time you've reached the end, you'll be well on your way to crafting arousing and exciting scenes that thrill each and every one of your readers.

Ashley Lister

Introducing the genre

1

WRITING SEX

'I'm talking about Parnell's story. Did it give you any ideas?'

Charlotte shrugged. 'It made me question the dubious mentality of our hosts and their guests. Or did you mean something other than that?'

Serena shook her head. They mounted the stairs and she pushed her sister into the shared bedroom before daring to raise her voice above a whisper. 'I want to try it.'

Charlotte rolled her eyes. 'Have you been mixing travel sickness pills and alcohol again?'

'I mean it. I want to try it.'

'No way.'

'Didn't the idea excite you? Didn't it give you a thrill thinking about it?'

'No.' Charlotte frowned and then asked, 'What idea?'

'The idea of being spanked beneath a full moon. Doesn't the thought send your pulse racing?'

Ashton, L., 'A Stout Length of Birch'

We read fiction to enjoy the experiences of fictional characters. In a good horror story, we enjoy the thrill of being frightened. In a good romance we savour the magic of love. And, in good erotica, we share the pleasure of a character's sexual excitement.

Erotica usually focuses on:

◆ the thrill of sexual experiences;

◆ the dynamics of sexual relationships;

◆ the mechanics of sexual interplay.

However, while erotica is thought to be all about the sex, it's often about a lot more than that. Over the following pages we'll look at how sex is currently being written, we'll look at some of the more popular ways of approaching sex in fiction and we'll consider some exercises to help writers craft successful erotic scenes.

EXERCISE

Think about all the erotic titles you've ever read and all the erotic scenes you've encountered in fiction. Try to decide what you liked about them. It doesn't matter whether critics would call them literary erotica or genre erotica or pornography. We'll look at those labels soon enough. What matters here is whether or not you enjoyed the story or the events being described. What matters is your reaction to the erotic content and the erotic interaction of the characters.

Keep a record of what works and what doesn't work within any erotic fiction you encounter. As we progress through this book you'll keep returning to these notes.

LITERARY EROTICA V. GENRE EROTICA

Euphrosine and Delbene were soon to offer me what I was seeking. Eager to undertake my education, the Superior one day invited me to luncheon. Euphrosine was there; the weather was incredibly warm, and this excessive ardour of the sun afforded them an excuse for the disarray I found them in: apart from an undergarment of transparent lawn maintained by nothing more than a large bow of pink ribbon, they were perfectly nude.

'Since you first arrived at this establishment,' Mme Delbene began, kissing me rather carelessly upon the forehead, her eye

and hand betraying a certain restlessness, 'I have had an unabating desire to make your intimate acquaintance. You are very attractive.'

Marquis de Sade, *Juliette*

Before starting to write any erotic story it's worth establishing some goals:

◆ Are you writing a story because you believe you can produce a work of literary erotica in the style of the Marquis De Sade, Nancy Friday, John Cleland or Leopold von Sacher-Masoch?

◆ Are you trying to produce a piece of genre erotica that will hopefully emulate the success of *The Story of O, The Happy Hooker, Belle de Jour* or *Fifty Shades of Grey?*

◆ Are you hoping to write personal fiction to simply titillate a partner with a raunchy shared fantasy?

There are no right or wrong answers to these questions. A writer might aim to achieve one, two or all three of these in the same story, although it's easier to approach them one at a time. In erotica all of these are viable goals even though there are no guarantees of literary acclaim or financial success or reader titillation. However, knowing why a story is being written is always a useful starting point.

The differences between these three types of writing make them fairly distinct.

◆ **Literary erotica** is usually the most critically respected of the erotic genres.

◆ Literary erotica tends to use an elevated language and style.

◆ Literary erotica will often show sex as being an unpleasant experience or an experience with negative repercussions. Oftentimes, literary erotica will show sex as being boring or disappointing or dissatisfying on some other level.

Justine, by the Marquis de Sade, is subtitled *The Misfortunes of Virtue*. Throughout *Justine*, every time the heroine makes a decision that should be seen as morally correct, events conspire to punish her with some act of sexual barbarism.

Juliette, the Marquis de Sade's story of Justine's sister, tells the story of a woman who embraces vice. Consequently she savours a happy life because she's abandoned virtue and piety. On the only occasion when Juliette does the morally correct thing in this novel she suffers repercussions for her actions.

Venus in Furs, by Leopold von Sacher-Masoch, is the story of a man who yearns to be subjected to sexual cruelty. He willingly subjects himself to misery in the name of erotic experimentation.

❛ It's obviously a huge oversimplification to say that literary erotica only ever deals with sex in a negative light. There are many titles that could be used to argue against this opinion. But more often than not, any work that is categorised as literary erotica does tend to fit this pattern. ❜

- ◆ **Genre erotica** is usually more accessible than literary erotica.

- ◆ Genre erotica tends to promote an ethos of social responsibility. Characters in genre erotica will rarely indulge in the use of recreational drugs and characters in erotica will practice safe sex whenever practicable and possible for the story.

- ◆ Genre erotica, particularly contemporary genre erotica, is usually more sex-positive than literary erotica. In genre erotica, characters enjoy the whole gamut of sexual experiences and go from one exciting liaison to another. Usually characters in genre erotica discover that each sexual adventure is more fulfilling than the previous one.

Consider the way Anastasia savours each encounter with Christian Grey in *Fifty Shades of Grey*. Even though conflicts develop within the story, the sex remains wholly satisfying for Anastasia and Christian.

In *The Story of O* by Pauline Réage, O is subjected to increasing levels of sexual discipline but her pleasure increases with each episode.

There are commercial reasons for these choices. Editors want readers to return and buy future books from their imprints. It's commonly believed that readers are more likely to return if they've enjoyed a happy story rather than a sad one. This response is the supply and demand aspect of filling that market need.

❝ Again, this is a massive generalisation but, as a rule of thumb guide, it's a useful way of separating literary and genre erotica. Modern editors with commercial priorities want to give readers stories that are filled with positive sexual experiences so that they'll come back for more. ❞

- **Personal fiction** is often written for the entertainment and arousal of lovers. These stories are usually the sexual recipes for what one partner wants to try with another.

- The commonest feature about personal fiction is that the focus is on sexual intimacy and there's little in the way of story to support the activities and interactions being described.

- Under this category we also find **Fan fiction**. This is an area of writing where stories are written by fans to include existing characters or settings. This is an area where Kirk and Spock can become intimately acquainted or where characters such as Bella, Edward and Jacob progress their intimacies to the next level.

While there is a thriving community of online writers producing Fan fiction, it must be remembered that the use of another writer's characters in fiction, especially in erotic fiction, can carry legal implications. Admittedly, some authors are happy for their work to be developed in this way. But there are other authors who will use the full weight of appropriate copyright laws to protect their creations.

❝ My own thoughts are, whilst there are some inspirational characters out there that make us (as readers) want to carry on living in their storyworld: it's our duty as writers to create new, original and engaging characters for our own readers. ❞

In this book the focus will be on the middle ground of well-written genre erotica. There will be regular references to literary erotica. There will also be a constant eye on ensuring the reader is aroused, as would befit personal fiction. To my mind, whether the writer intended a piece to be genre erotica or literary erotica, if the reader isn't aroused then it's not really erotic.

EXERCISE

Answer the questions already mentioned in this section:

Do you want to add to the canon of literary erotica?
Do you want to produce the next genre erotica bestseller?
Do you want to provide a special thrill for a small but important readership?

As was said before – there are no right or wrong answers. It's easier to maintain focus on just one of these goals. It's possible to answer YES to all three questions: but which one of these three is the most important to you? We all have different goals with our writing. All that's important is identifying what type of erotica you want to produce.

THE RIGHT RUDE WORDS

'C'mon folks, I'll rack 'em up again. See how Cal, here, got one right in there? Popped that cherry good? Here y'go, show us what y'got.' I caught just enough movement to know she was tossing her long dark hair and twitching her hips for emphasis. 'Stick that ol' dart right in! Ri-i-i-ght in there'!

'Right in where?' asked a wise guy. 'Show me again'!

'If you can't find the spot on your own, hot stuff,' she shot back, 'maybe you better go home and practice some more on your favourite sheep.'

Green, S., 'Pulling'

Erotica is often wrongly associated with a need for rude words. It's fair to say that erotica does use a distinctive vocabulary. Readers often come to erotica looking for graphic descriptions of sexual arousal. Those same readers expect to encounter well-crafted scenes of physical intimacy. Consequently, writers need an appropriate language to label those particular body parts and to accurately describe what those body parts are doing. However, because many of these terms are commonly associated with taboo language, some writers struggle to work comfortably in this genre.

❛ The rudest words in contemporary English refer to sex acts, parts of the body and bodily waste. Historically taboo words have been associated with religion and illness, although these terms are no longer considered so offensive. ❜

Erotica doesn't really need any rude words. If colourful language is used in erotica it only ever accounts for a very small proportion of the overall content. The most essential thing to remember is that all words, rude or not, should be appropriate in the following contexts. They should be:

- appropriate for character;
- appropriate for the story being told;
- appropriate for the author;
- appropriate for the audience.

Appropriate for character
We'll explore more about character and dialogue in later chapters. However, it's worth considering here that characters should always use appropriate words.

- A medical expert and authority on all matters sexual is not going to discuss his 'thingy' and her 'lady pocket'.
- A Regency period hero is unlikely to discuss the 'rocket in his pants'.
- The lady's maid he's courting is never going to say she's been accessed in more places than wi-fi.

These are obvious anomalies and anachronisms. But they illustrate a point about the words that characters are likely to use. Depending on background, personality and their attitudes to sex, characters will have different sexual vocabularies. This point will be discussed further when we look at describing characters through speech.

Appropriate for the story being told

In a gentle romance, the narrator is more likely to use a softer vocabulary than would be encountered in a story of hardcore, graphic BDSM. Again, this is not about one group of words being *better* than another: it's all about using a language that's appropriate for the story being told.

Appropriate for the author

As authors we only need use the words that are appropriate for the storyworlds that we've created. No one can force us to use words that we dislike. No one can force us to use words that don't convey the exact sentiment we want to express. Some authors avoid all taboo language in their writing and still tell a compelling erotic tale. Others use a full lexicon of swearwords to achieve the same affect. Neither way is wrong or right as long as the author is happy with the finished story.

Appropriate for the audience

It's difficult to tell what will work for an audience and what won't. Often, by the time a story has reached its intended audience, it's too late for an author to change words. The best indicator here is the opinions of editors who have a clear idea of what readers expect.

> ❝ One of my favourite editors refuses to accept work that includes the word 'pussy' to identify female genitalia. Another editor I've worked with advised writers to change the word 'cock' to 'prick' whenever possible because he thought it was more aesthetically pleasing. ❞

This is not to suggest that an author should always bow to the demands of an editor. Each of us has a clear idea of what readers deem acceptable but that doesn't mean authors or editors will always be correct. As writers, all we can do is use a vocabulary that we feel justified in presenting to our readership.

EXERCISE

Create three lists with the following headings:

MALE
FEMALE
SEX ACTS

Under each of the headings write down a list of all the words that could be used to describe male body parts, female body parts or sexual acts *that are appropriate for your writing*. Write down all the words you can think of. Cross out the words you would not want to use within your writing. Keep this list safe.

READERS AND WRITERS

One of the first questions writers of erotica get asked is, 'Have you done all the things you've written about?' It should be noted here that only authors of erotica get asked this question.

- No one asks science fiction authors which planets they've visited.

- No one asks children's story writers if they've ever encountered a real hungry caterpillar, or a genuine talking bear.

- No one asks the authors of murder mysteries if they've ever killed a person.

Yet, when an author writes an erotic scene, many readers assume the author is only capable of writing about sexual experiences they've enjoyed or those sexual fantasies they would like to see made real. Very few readers can accept that the author of erotic fiction, like the author of every other type of genre fiction, is most commonly a writer involved in the act of telling a story.

This can be problematic for some writers and it's an issue that should be addressed early in any writer's career. A similar issue is the common group of fears that stop some writers from tackling erotic fiction and sex scenes. Many authors avoid writing sex scenes because:

- They worry that family (mother/father/auntie/grandma) will read the story and assume they're related to a deviant.

- They worry that friends and colleagues will read their story and assume they're acquainted with a pervert.

- They worry that employers will read their work and use it as grounds to show that a person is not suitable for employment.

These fears are not unjustified. I have spoken with writers whose parents have been horrified to discover that their child was involved in writing something as obscene as erotic fiction. I have personally had a work colleague stop me in a corridor to tell me that all my writing was pure filth (even though she'd never read a word of my fiction: she only knew the genre). I know of several writers who've been surreptitiously warned by their employers to stop writing erotica under their own names or it might have an adverse effect on their employment.

> ❛ Obviously this is not the case every time. I have more supportive colleagues than unsupportive colleagues and my family are proud of my accomplishments as a writer. But I also use pseudonyms for a lot of my writing. I do this so my name is not solely associated with explicit material. And I do this so I can write for a range of markets without always being associated with the preconceived ideas of readers who might be influenced by their own ignorance and prejudice. ❜

The most practical pieces of advice here are:

- Always be comfortable with the material you're writing. Don't publish anything that you'd be embarrassed to call your own.

- Be careful who knows about the relationship between you and your writing.

I'd love to advocate a 'publish and be damned' approach but there are enough people with prejudices and personal agendas to make this attitude dangerous.

EXERCISE

Would you feel safe and comfortable sharing your writing? How do you think family, friends and employers would respond if you penned a racy piece of fiction? If you sincerely believe everyone would be happy for your achievement, then congratulate yourself on having found a sage selection of friends, etc. who support your endeavours.

If you think that any of your acquaintances might make your life uncomfortable because you've written and published something of an adult nature, then you might want to consider using a pseudonym and being selective about who knows that you're an author.

SUMMARY

- ◆ Erotic fiction focuses on exciting a sexual response from the reader.
  - ◇ Literary erotica often includes a level of grim realism.
  - ◇ Genre erotica is more likely to have a sex-positive content.
  - ◇ Personal erotica is usually written to titillate.

- ◆ Chose your words appropriately. Make sure they are:
  - ◇ appropriate for specific characters;
  - ◇ appropriate for the story you're telling;
  - ◇ appropriate for your voice as an author;
  - ◇ appropriate for the readership.

- ◆ Be judicious about who knows that you're writing raunchy material.

Virginia Woolf famously said: 'Writing is like sex. First you do it for love, then you do it for your friends, and then you do it for money.' Regardless of whether you're writing for love, friends or money, it's worth knowing which genre your work would best suit, understanding about using an appropriate vocabulary for your intended readership, and being aware that readers don't always understand that writers sometimes use their imagination for storytelling.

Understanding the ground rules

2

FOLLOWING THE RULES OF WRITING EROTICA

'Yes. All right.'

He caressed her shoulder gently as they walked. 'Maia, if you move in with me, I'm going to keep you like an animal on a very short tether. You'll have no autonomy at all in that house. Not much outside of it. Remember there'll be constant restraints, rules, humiliations, punishments. All the time, do you understand? You're not going to draw a free breath.'

She was trembling beneath his arm. He held her more firmly and kept her moving.

'Following rules doesn't mean you'll know what's coming either . . .'

Jacob, A., *As She's Told*

There are more rules governing erotica than are applied to any other genre. However, as our male protagonist Anders says in this passage: *following rules doesn't mean you'll know what's coming.*

As with all rules, the following are not written in stone. Many writers break them more often than they observe them. However, it's worth noting the rules to see how some writers have used them to good effect. It's also useful to know which rules are in place before we attempt to break them.

Rules for erotica can be grouped under the following general headers:

- ◆ Touching taboo subjects

- ◆ Researching sex scenes:
  - ◇ Personal experience
  - ◇ Reading adult literature
  - ◇ Watching adult films

Touching taboo subjects

When I was sixteen my mom confessed to me that she had a vibrator, which a friend had given to her, but which she never used. She just liked to keep it around 'for laughs.'

Within a day I found the vibrator and immediately plunged it into my own ass while in a fit of vigorous masturbation. I could spend the rest of my life in analysis and never get to the bottom of that one.

Keck, K., *Oedipus Wrecked*

There are some subjects that the majority of genre erotica publishers won't accept. The main five are:

- ◆ incest;

- ◆ sex involving underage participants;

- ◆ non-consensual sex;

- ◆ bestiality;

- ◆ necrophilia.

This is not to say that no one ever writes stories about these subjects. These themes do appear in some erotica but they're more commonly found as dark elements of other genres, either with or without erotic connotations.

Incest has been presented in dramas since *Oedipus Rex*. It continues to be a recurring theme in contemporary soap operas and modern-day crime thrillers. But it's seldom accepted in genre erotica.

Sex involving underage participants, as well as **non-consensual sex**, is the mainstay of misery memoirs and tragic child abuse diaries. Again, these themes are also common in murder mysteries where such acts are used to justify motives. But they're rarely touched by the mainstream publishers of genre erotica.

Paranormal romances, especially those including vampires, werewolves and their human lovers, continue to blur the boundaries between what is **bestiality** and **necrophilia** and what is an extended fantasy of modern romance. However, it's unlikely that any contemporary genre erotica publisher would consider a title that touched on themes of human/animal interaction or a scene where a living person sexually desecrated a corpse. These acts are more indicative of serious mental health issues rather than being suggestive, daring or exciting.

This list is not exhaustive and it's worth bearing in mind that all publishers are different.

◆ Some publishers refuse to consider material with scatological content (stories where sexual pleasure is associated with urine or faeces). Other publishers happily accept such stories.

◆ Some publishers don't want submissions that include references to pain or blood. Other publishers are comfortable with these subjects.

◆ For most publishers, because we all have subjective views of propriety, there will be subjects that they don't feel appropriate for treatment in erotic fiction.

❝ It's worth remembering that different publishers know their readers are turned on by different things. A successful writer will take these considerations to heart, learn the requirements of those different publishers and pitch their material to the right market. ❞

Obviously we live in a world with freedoms of speech where any writer can craft a story that touches any of the above themes as well as darker ones that aren't mentioned here. It's noted that these themes could all be addressed in literary erotica with its emphasis on the more realistic aspects of sex. However, for a writer attempting to make a breakthrough with their first genre erotica piece, it's unlikely that she or he will find a publisher willing to work with a text covering one of the aforementioned themes.

EXERCISE

Produce a list of subjects you wouldn't want to deal with in an erotic context. Just as we all have things that we find exciting, we all have things that we consider a complete turn-off. Produce a list of subjects that you don't want to write about. Keep the list safe and be prepared to add to it and modify the content as you write more erotica.

While you're working on lists, produce a list of subjects you *would* want to write about. This will be useful for our next topic where we look at research.

Researching through discussion, reading and adult films

Instruction in sex is as important as instruction in food; yet not only are our adolescents not taught the physiology of sex, but never warned that the strongest sexual attraction may exist between persons so incompatible in tastes and capacities that they could not endure living together for a week much less a lifetime.

George Bernard Shaw

Bernard Shaw's thoughts on sex education apply equally to instruction in writing about sex. Research is important for writers regardless of genre. It's essential for writers of erotica because writing about erotica touches on a subject that many people are reluctant to discuss.

❝ The walls of every creative writing class echo with the cries of 'Write what you know.' It's a saying that gets repeated until it stops making sense. But writing what you know can be quite limiting for anyone wanting to write erotica. Is it possible for one writer to know about every sexual act? This is where writers turn to research. ❞

Research in erotica usually falls under the following headings:

- Experience
  - Personal
  - Anecdotal

- Reading

- Watching adult films

Experience – personal and anecdotal

When they finally broke apart both of them were gasping.

'Before we do anything else,' Lisa began, 'I have to tell you that I work to the twenty minute rule. You don't have a problem with that, do you?'

'The twenty minute rule?'

'I never stay with any man for longer than twenty minutes at a party,' she explained. 'Twenty minutes from now I'm going to kiss you goodbye and thank you for your time, and then I'm either going to go and find my husband, or I'll find another man to spend twenty minutes with.'

His fingers lingered against her bare arm.

Lister, A., 'The Twenty-Minute Rule'

❝ The passage above comes from a short story I wrote for *Swing!*, Jolie Du Pré's anthology of fiction about sexual swingers. The idea for the story came to me while I was researching a non-fiction book on swinging couples in the UK. At the time I'd been talking with a lady who explained that she got the most from her evenings when she set a half-hour limit with each person she met at a party. It was a condition that was not dissimilar to the one mentioned in the story I eventually wrote. The idea of a self-imposed restriction, especially a restriction in the hedonistic abandon of an erotic sex party, struck me as unusual enough to qualify for an interesting story. ❞

As was mentioned previously, one of the first questions writers of erotica get asked is, 'Have you done all the things you've written about?' Personally I have neither the time nor the anatomical capabilities to have done all the things I've written about. I've written about things I could never physically experience. I'm a man, and have always been a man, so when I've written about pleasure from a female perspective it's not something I've personally experienced.

However, I discuss sex with my partner. I talk with friends who share anecdotes. I discuss sex with colleagues. I talk sex with editors and fellow writers. We chat about sexual literature and we argue about what works and what doesn't work in the real world with real people.

Obviously I don't talk about sex with people who don't want to talk sex. But when I'm dealing with fellow professionals who feel confident expressing opinions about these personal subjects, I take full advantage of their knowledge and experience.

EXERCISE

Consider any of the anecdotes that friends or acquaintances have shared about their sex lives. Reflect on one story that you think might work as part of an erotic narrative. Change enough details (names, location, physical description, etc.) so there's no chance of causing any potential embarrassment. Fill in the erotic detail to make the story sexually exciting and explicit. Write the anecdote as a piece of personal fiction.

Reading

And just as he was starting to let his guard down, he said, 'I guess I'd better get home. My puppy will be waiting for me.' No mention of a woman. 'It was nice talking to you,' he mumbled, turning to walk away.

'Hey wait,' I called after him. 'Have you heard about the new book club that is starting up next month? Mystery novels only, I hear.'

'No, I haven't. Are you going?' His eyes lit up.

'Sure.' I needed to see him again because, unlike lots of other men I'd met, he had both a penis and a brain. 'Actually, I'm running it.' It was a lie. In fact, there was no book club – the words had just come flying out.

'Sounds good. I'll watch for the flyers. See you later.' With that, he was gone.

Fox, A., 'Once You Go Black'

Reading is essential to being a writer. For anyone wanting to write erotica you need to read erotica whenever possible. Seeing how other writers present sex on the page is the clearest way of seeing what works and understanding what doesn't work.

Read the following:

- Read titles that you find entertaining.

- Read titles that you think might be too literary to be enjoyable.

- Read titles that you think might be too salacious to have any merit.

- Read – and acknowledge what works and what doesn't work.

❛ I was once interviewed on the radio as part of a panel of experts discussing poetry. One of the panel members said, "I don't read poetry. I only write it."

This lack of involvement in his chosen genre showed in the quality of his work. His writing was unremarkable, unimpressive and mostly inaccessible. It was not based on an understanding of contemporary or proven approaches to the subject. It also made me wonder why he thought people would want to listen to his poetry when he didn't care to listen to anyone else's work. ❜

Reading can also provide writers with inspiration for erotic stories.

- Read agony aunt columns where people write to newspapers and magazines with the sorts of dilemmas that would make fascinating novels in their own right:

My girlfriend is having an affair with my wife: what should I do?

I've fallen in love with my boss but he doesn't notice me: how can I make him leave his civil partner?

◆ Read medical research papers on studies of pleasure, sex and sexuality. None of us knows everything about sex. Becoming a 'sexpert', or at least being an educated amateur, will increase the tone of authority in your writing.

◆ Read kiss-and-tell stories in the tabloids to see what's supposedly happening in the bedrooms of celebrities. Reflect on these allegedly true stories and decide which you think are sexually arousing and which would be unlikely to work in the type of erotica you want to create. Incorporate the useful material into your writing and leave out the details that don't appeal to you.

EXERCISE

Select any tabloid with a racy headline about love rats, two-timers or luxurious nights of passion. Read the story and consider how the raw elements could be used in a piece of fiction.

Make notes of the character types involved (e.g. sexually voracious football player, busty model, popular musician, record producer, TV executive, etc.).

Make notes on how the story develops and rewrite this as a piece of erotica. Change enough details so there's no chance of causing any potential embarrassment. Change the names of all participants and locations. Fill in the erotic detail to make the story sexually exciting and explicit.

Watching adult films

Most adult films appear to rely on a predictable LA formula: Barbie gets banged by Ken while both recite trite banter referencing either the size of Ken's manhood or the tightness of Barbie's holes. All of that happens on a shoddily art-directed set with no plot and bad makeup. Either that, or it's too softcore, like watching a Lifetime original movie with exposed nipples.

But while porn bores me, porn stars fascinate me. Most people spend their whole lives trying to please their parents, whereas porn stars are people who've openly given up. They're kind of like people with facial tattoos.

I figured, if I worked on the set of a porno for a day, I would get to meet porn stars. Plus, I would gain experience for future filmmaking endeavours.

Reverend Jen Miller, *Live Nude Elf*

Reverend Jen Miller makes a strong argument against pornography in the passage above. She's right to point out that such films usually set unrealistic expectations for sex. It's fair to say that the following features occur in the majority of contemporary adult films:

◆ Orgasms are assured and almost instantaneous.

◆ Erections are substantial and unfailing.

◆ Pleasure is noisy, guaranteed and surprisingly visual.

However, while it's acknowledged that adult films do depict an idealised version of sex, access to adult films can be useful for those who require any additional visual prompts for the imagination. Miller is correct that most pornographic movies have little plot and risible dialogue. But writers can take their inspiration from many sources and the writers of erotica would be foolish to overlook the inspiration of adult films.

EXERCISE

You're writing a story about a couple at a dinner party. Your main character thinks that the host's new partner looks just like the star of an adult film. How does this character convey her/his suspicion to her/his partner? Do either of them dare ask the host's new partner if s/he has enjoyed an acting career? What answer are they expecting? How does the scene develop once they get their answer?

SUMMARY

- In genre erotica, avoid the five main taboos:
  - incest;
  - underage sex;
  - non-consensual sex;
  - bestiality;
  - necrophilia.

- Research thoroughly using:
  - personal experience;
  - experiences of colleagues and acquaintances;
  - extensive reading;
  - adult films.

All writing should be enjoyable for the writer. The subject matter should be a pleasure to research because it's something that the writer already enjoys considering. If you're writing about a subject that doesn't interest or excite you then it's apparent you're working in the wrong genre.

Learning the basics

3

THE STORYTELLER AND THE READER

An alarm was beeping and lights were flashing.

Vanessa jerked awake. She'd been dreaming that she and Kashika had been racing as girl ponies. They'd just won the Grand National and the Queen had been about to pin rosettes on their breasts . . .

The bedroom screen was flashing an urgent red and sounding the alarm. She fumbled for the bedside light switch. The glowing numerals of her clock radio showed it was twenty past five.

She found the remote and pointed it at the screen. An image appeared of a slender woman, perhaps in her mid-fifties, with a strong straight nose and a narrow intelligent unlined face. Her bright blue eyes were keen and commanding.

'Sorry to wake you, Vanessa, but this is urgent,' the woman said.
Arden, A., The Girlflesh Captives

Using the right point of view is vital for telling a story. Handled properly, point of view becomes virtually invisible. Used effectively it can add new layers to a story. And, handled badly, it can be intrusive, spoil the mood of a piece and stop the reader from enjoying an otherwise entertaining tale.

❛ Point of view involves little more than knowing which characters are telling a story. Well-crafted point of view only involves
being   sure   the   story   is   told   from   a   consistent   perspective.

❜

Imagine you are going to rewrite the Grimm Brothers' 1812 story
of Little Snow-White as an erotic fairy tale. This is the story on
which the animated film was based but there are substantial
differences.

◆ In the original story we aren't given character names for the
  dwarves.

◆ In the original story the villain is Little Snow-White's mother
  (referred to as her *godless mother*) and not her stepmother.

◆ In the original story, Little Snow-White is revived from a
  deathlike stupor when a servant of the prince smacks her on
  the back and dislodges the lump of poisoned apple that was
  stuck in her throat.

We'll worry about the erotic content later. For now we want to
concentrate on point of view and perspective. Consequently the
following points need to be considered.

◆ Do you write the story from Little Snow-White's perspective?

◆ Little Snow-White is the central character. It would make sense
  to see events from her point of view as we are telling her story.

◆ Could you write the story from the perspective of one of the
  dwarves? It will be a unique approach and will allow the
  narration to continue even while Little Snow-White is lying
  unconscious in her glass coffin.

◆ Would it be possible to write the story from the point of view
  of the prince? The prince only appears in the final act of this
  story, so it might be difficult to see the whole story from his
  perspective.

◆ Could you give the story a dark twist and tell it from the point
  of view of Little Snow-White's godless mother? This character's perspective would certainly be exciting and innovative.

All of these points of view, and more, are possible. But a writer needs to carefully select point of view to effectively tell the right story. By considering different narrators, even if the events of the story are identical, the focus of the story being told will change in many subtle and different ways.

Told from Little Snow-White's point of view we're going to experience all the highs and lows of the story as she is exiled, helped by the dwarves, and then wins the heart of a prince and triumphs over her godless mother. But there will be a missing part in the final third of the story where Little Snow-White is in a coma.

Told from the point of view of the godless mother, the story will have a sad ending and will be narrated by a very different character from the pure and innocent Little Snow-White. In the ending to the Grimm version of the fairy tale, iron shoes are heated on a fire until they glow. The godless mother is then forced to wear the heated shoes, which burn her feet, and she then has to dance herself to death.

> Many readers are surprised by the gruesome and grisly developments within original fairy stories. Because we associate these tales so strongly with children's stories we forget that the original material was not dedicated to a specific audience of minors. They include scenes of horrific cruelty and brutality.

Point of view should remain single and consistent whenever possible. If a story starts from Little Snow-White's point of view, it needs to continue being narrated from that perspective. If the narrative voice has to change – if the reader needs to see what's happening at the prince's castle, or if the storyteller wants us to watch the godless mother talking to her mirror – then a chapter break is needed so the reader isn't confused by the shift in perspectives.

Typically point of view is divided into four traditional perspectives:

◆ first person;

◆ second person;

- third person;

- omniscient.

Of these four perspectives the commonest nowadays are **first person** and **third person** but examples of all four are considered on the following pages.

First person

I shrugged. Rebecca didn't date. She lived behind her camera lens, taking pictures and making judgements. And if that was enough for her, then I wished her well. But I needed more in my world. I needed Marlon to fuck me while patrons watched Sid and Nancy *or* Last Tango in Paris, *or any one of the many mostly depressing second-run movies that we played. Then, I needed Jarred to take me again, in the morning, when we were fresh faced and Ivory scented and ready for Sunday brunch and walks in Griffith Park.*

I wanted different things from my different men. Couldn't Rebecca understand that?

Tyler, A., 'Some Like it Hot'

In the first person point of view, the narrator talks directly to the reader. In the example above the narrator tells her story straight to the reader. We are left in no doubt as to who is the central character here. And we can be confident that everything that happens will be related to this narrator/character in some way.

- The passage opens with a reference to the narrator's physical actions: *I shrugged.*

- The reader is given the narrator's opinion of Rebecca.

- The narrator reveals her explicit desires for Marlon and Jarred.

- The reader is never in any doubt about who is telling this story as the narrator explains her wants, her needs and her desires.

There are advantages and disadvantages to using first person point of view. It's worth weighing their potential benefits before beginning any writing project.

Advantages

◆ There is an immediacy to a first-person narration.

◆ Readers are taken directly into the storyworld with the central character.

◆ Readers enjoy all the story's experiences alongside that central character.

These features can be quite compelling in erotica. The reader is being told explicit details by a character who is actively involved in the intimacy of the story. It's almost as though the fictional character is sharing his or her secrets with the reader.

Disadvantages

◆ First person is a restricted point of view. The narrator can only reveal information that is known to the central character.

◆ The narrator needs to have a voice that the reader finds sympathetic.

◆ If a reader has no empathy with the narrator, the story will not be engaging.

Many of my writing students shy away from first person because they dislike repeating the word 'I'. Repeating any word seems like bad writing and repeating the word 'I' can come across as clumsy. But the word 'I' doesn't need to be repeated to excess in first-person point of view. Consider the following first-person narration and look how long it takes for the narrator to use 'I'.

It was after three in the morning when the show was over. We packed up our instruments, content that we had done our best, earned our bread. The owner of the Club Nutty, a speakeasy on the city's swanky shore, invited us back to his penthouse place overlooking the ships and the glittering lake. We knew better than to refuse his offer. Flanked by his gunmen, he told us that he had some people over there, and that we could pick up some more cash if we stuck around.

One of Mr Danton's bodyguards, with his gun in plain view, slung the girl into our sedan, a female with the colour of a dark plum. She smiled at me and started going through her purse. The hood shoved two more girls on top of us, cursed at them and slammed the door.

It was hot as hell. The kind of heat that made your skin stick to your clothes. I was burning up.

Riley, C., 'It's Tight Like That'

In this passage Riley's narrator refers to *we*, *us* and *our* as the story begins, talking about the members of a band of speakeasy musicians. Again, it's hard for the writer to get away from personal pronouns. But this story is not repeatedly using the word 'I'. And, as readers, we're treated to a personal story from the perspective of a character intimately involved with the events. Who could ask for more than that with an erotic story?

EXERCISE

Write a short erotic scene in the first person.

In the scene you are about to write, the narrator/character should be on the phone with a lover, discussing a dinner date they have planned. Begin with the words, 'I picked up the phone on the third ring . . .' Keep every detail from the perspective of the narrator/character.

Third person

The second book had been even more extreme than the first, and the pictures in it acted on her system like a drug. A powerful aphrodisiac to be exact. The more she looked at naked, punished bottoms, complicated systems of bondage and perverted unnatural penetrations, the more the pit of her belly ached and the wetter and wetter her sex became. It was lust in a way she'd never felt before; certainly not a bit like the mild tingle she'd occasionally felt when she fancied a handsome man. Although she did admit that when she'd ogled that photo spread of Lukas, he'd definitely had an effect on her. When she'd thought about Roger, there'd never even been a twinge . . .

Starr, D., Designed for Sin

In third person the narrator describes the world as it is seen by the central character. But the narrator is not the central character. The narrator never says, 'I thought this' or 'we did that'. Instead the narrator consistently refers to the central character as 'he' or 'she' or by their name.

To some extent this point of view lacks the intimacy of first-person perspectives. It is also restricted by the same limits of only showing us what that central character can perceive.

> ❝ In classes, I refer to third person as *parrot perspective*. This is a story that could be narrated by a parrot sitting on the central character's shoulder. We're not being told the story by the central character. We're only being told the story from the perspective of the character. It's a subtle but important difference. ❞

Although third person lacks the immediacy and intimacy of first person, it has lots of advantages.

- Because the narrator of a third-person perspective is not a character, it's possible for the reader to be told more about a character.

- The narrator can describe all characters from an objective perspective.

- The central character can come across as natural rather than an obsessive intent on cataloguing every detail that's relevant to the story.

Third-person perspective remains the most popular point of view in contemporary fiction so it's not to be overlooked.

EXERCISE

Using third-person point of view, rewrite the scene from the previous exercise. Remove all traces of the first person and replace it with 'she' or 'he' references or direct references to the character's name.

Read the two scenes side by side and note the differences. While first person does have a greater degree of intimacy, third person will likely allow for more detail to be given.

Write a new third-person scene showing those two characters meeting for the date they've planned. Use third-person perspective for only one character and show the couple flirting throughout their meal.

Second person

Here you are: nervous, waiting for her to arrive, wearing the evening dress, thong and stockings that she has sent; crossing and re-crossing your legs. You have turned off most of the lights in your small flat preferring darkness.

All you know is that she has told you that the two of you will be going out tonight. You do not know where. She will pick you up at the appropriate time. You are trying not to think too hard about the night ahead; you recall the last time she picked you up and took you out in London at night. That was the time with the blindfold so you didn't see much of where you were in the city or how you got there. But every time you remember a part of that night your stomach clenches. She shamed you.

Grey, V., 'Shame Game'

❝ After discussing first- and third-person perspectives, students often ask about second person. Second person is possibly the most intimate of all perspectives because the reader is the central character. However, because it's such an unusual way of writing (and reading), it's not particularly common in contemporary fiction. When it's used effectively, second person can be far more powerful than any other point of view. ❞

The narrator in the second person constantly refers to 'you' in this story – you the central character. The narrator does not use any first-person forms of address because the narrator is not in this story. Instead, the narrator simply tells a character (you) what you did in this story and how much you enjoyed it.

It's one of the most difficult points of view for any writer to approach because it's such an unnatural way of telling a story. If I was writing a story about how 'you' had enjoyed an adventure it wouldn't seem right for me to tell you what you did. I would assume that you already knew what you'd done, so the story seems somewhat redundant.

Also, because second-person narratives are so uncommon, it's difficult for a reader to approach the text without being distracted by the way the story is being told.

Second person is more commonly associated with writing recipes, giving road directions and playing interactive adventure games.

Second person also becomes confusing because it raises issues about perspective and the relationship between the reader and the text.

◆ Am I really the central character in this story?

Obviously not because the writer is describing events that I don't recall experiencing.

◆ Am I reading a story that is a retelling of events that happened to some other intended reader?

That's a possibility. And, if that's the case, then the author has moved the narrative onto a new level of discourse.

◆ If the central character in the story is a different gender from the reader, will this make the story more or less exciting?

Second person is not common in fiction. When it has been used it's often been associated with experimental writing. However, it can be particularly dramatic and effective when used within erotica because it's incorporating the reader directly into the centre of the action. If you enjoy writing in second person, keep experimenting with it. If you don't like second person, you will not be the first writer to decide to give it a miss.

EXERCISE

Take one of the characters from a scene used before and write a passage for them in second person. Avoid any reference to the first person. Describe what this character is doing, constantly referring to her or him as 'you'.

Note how this different tone affects your voice as a writer. Be aware that this can often feel more like 'telling' a story rather than 'showing' how the action develops.

Omniscient

There were two sisters very unlike each other. The elder, Juliette, was not yet sixteen, but already was as worldly-wise and sly as a woman of thirty. Moreover, she was inordinately vain, and frivolous and bold. Her firm supple figure and fine dark eyes lent her an attractiveness which was too soon brought to her own attention, and she had all the makings of a consummate coquette. On the other hand, Justine, her younger sister, was a modest, timid and ingenuous young creature; and just as Juliet was gay, wanton and unprincipled, so Justine was serious, melancholy and profuse with fine upright sentiments. But Justine was far less precocious; and her artless simplicity led her into many snares and pitfalls.

Marquis de Sade, *Justine*

In the passage above we are told that the two sisters are very unlike each other.

◆ We are given subjective judgements on Juliette's absence of morality and Justine's virtue.

◆ We are told that Juliette is: *as sly as a woman of thirty.*

◆ We are told Juliette is: *inordinately vain and frivolous and bold.*

All of this comes from the story's omniscient narrator who is telling the story to prove a point.

❝ This style of narration, from a narrator who appears to know everything, makes it very difficult for the reader to empathise with any particular character. More commonly it is now associated with an old-fashioned style of storytelling that has long since gone out of vogue. ❞

Carrie was being sent to Paris to complete her education. She was not pure Cuban, as there was a lot of Yankee blood on her father's side, but she had great, lustrous Spanish eyes, which gleamed as they fixed on the naked apparition of Hony. At the hotel, Lady Tittle having run down to Newport for the night, Hony and Carrie had shared a bed for company's sake – well . . . to continue.

Carrie was very dark and very slight. Her figure was really too slim to be good, but there was a feline grace in it which was very tempting. Her face lacked good features but her very full red lips, her glorious eyes, and her abundance of raven hair made up for any defects. She was a striking contrast to the pink and white beauty of golden-haired Hony.

Anon., *Pleasure Bound: Afloat*

In this passage we're told:

- Carrie's figure *was really too slim to be good.*
- It's suggested that: *Her face lacked good features.*
- Some features, lips, eyes and hair, *made up for any defects.*
- Her figure has *a feline grace which was very tempting.*

These judgements are given as facts, even though they're obviously the opinions of the anonymous omniscient narrator. We're not told who has decided that Carrie's face lacks good features. We're not told how her lips, eyes and hair make up for any defects. We're not told who it is who thinks her feline grace is tempting. We're simply told that these things are and asked to believe them.

The omniscient narrator has fallen out of fashion over the past few decades. This is possibly because this style of narration is more commonly associated with the traits of *telling* a story rather than *showing* detail. The omniscient narrator has a godlike knowledge of everyone and everything related to the story.

In both of these passages, the omniscient narrator gives the information to the reader, rather than trusting the reader to understand layers of subtext.

EXERCISE

Experiment briefly with *telling* a story instead of *showing* detail.

Tell a reader about two characters meeting.

Tell the reader how each character feels.

Tell the reader how events will transpire.

Read this work back. Does this allow the reader to sympathise with the characters? Does this feel as though the reader could be immersed in a convincing storyworld? Or are events just being relayed without trusting the reader to interpret actions and events?

SUMMARY

Fashions in writing come and go, so it's unlikely that the omniscient or the second person narrator will disappear forever. However, at the moment, neither is particularly common on the erotica bookshelves.

- Choose your narrative point of view wisely.
- Show details to your reader: don't tell them the story.
- Make sure your narrator will engage your reader.
- Don't change narrators halfway through a scene.

Whether a writer is using first person, second person or third person, the point of view should always be from the same character's perspective. If a different viewpoint is needed, a writer should start a new chapter from the perspective of a different character. Within a chapter, or within any unbroken passage of text, a shift in point of view will confuse the reader.

4

Creating convincing characters

THE IMPORTANCE OF STRONG CHARACTERS

Characters are possibly the most essential element in general fiction. This is particularly true for erotic fiction.

- Readers want to meet interesting and exciting characters.

- Readers want to invest in the adventures of characters who are believable.

- Readers want to enjoy the adventures and challenges faced by those characters.

- Readers of erotic fiction want to witness and share the sensual experiences of the characters contained in the story.

> ❛ No doubt there are some successful stories that contain no characters. In writing there are exceptions to every rule. However, exceptions aside, it's hard to understate the value of strong central characters in fiction. ❜

The use of character names for titles has been consistently exploited by authors of erotic literature.

- The Marquis de Sade's titles include *Justine*, with its sequel, *Juliette*.

◆ Leopold von Sacher-Masoch's *Venus in Furs* refers directly to the novel's antagonist.

◆ John Cleland's *Memoirs of a Woman of Pleasure* is better known as *Fanny Hill.*

◆ Pauline Réage's *Story of O* refers to the story's protagonist, O.

The title of any piece of fiction has several important roles.

◆ It acts as a label for the story.

◆ It reflects the content.

◆ It's used as a sales tool.

The fact that a character's name is so often used as the title shows the immense importance of characters within fiction.

EXERCISE

Write down a list of ten names: five female and five male. Make the names original. Try not to use the names of family, friends or celebrities. Pick names that you think sound interesting, exciting and believable. Keep the list safe because it will be needed for the next exercise.

NAMING CHARACTERS

Mr New York, Action Man, the Scottish Antonio Banderas, the French Gigolo, the Danish Pastry, Tantric Andy, Opera Man, and on and on. And on. I rarely call them by their names. My friend Michelle says my men shouldn't get a name until I've slept with them three times and, using her criteria, most of them remain nameless. That doesn't bother me. I'm not looking for a boyfriend. I'm looking for sex. It's my weekend retreat.
Portnoy, S., *The Butcher, The Baker, The Candlestick Maker*

In the real world the relationship between name and personality is curious. The majority of us live with names given to us either from before we were born, or from when we were too young to have established any personality traits. Yet it's surprising how often certain names suggest specific types of people. It's more surprising how often those suggested types are accurate. This relationship between the person and their name is even more important in the world of fiction.

◆ Rupert conjures up images of a wealthy individual with an Oxbridge background and a BBC English accent.

◆ Nikki, with its modern spelling, suggests someone youthful, vibrant and exciting.

◆ Agatha brings to mind an elderly matriarch.

◆ Jack is the name of a likeable rogue.

Obviously, the associations with these names change for anyone who is closely acquainted with a Rupert, Nikki, Agatha or Jack, or anyone who is known by one of those names. But, for the rest of us, these names (and many others) conjure up immediate personality types

---

❛ In erotic fiction many new writers are tempted to select comical names with lewd humour at their centre. Jenny Talia, Fanny Rash, Dick Cummings and Eric Shun are names that can titillate. But this humour is likely to break the reader's suspension of disbelief and diminish the effectiveness of the fiction. We read about characters and expect them to be based in some sort of reality that resembles the world we inhabit. If there is a world where Mr and Mrs Rash elect to name their daughter Fanny, it's to be hoped it's nothing like the reality the rest of us inhabit. With the exception of the James Bond and Austen Powers films, with characters such as *Pussy Galore* and *Felicity Shagwell*, character names in fiction are usually kept to a level of realism that does not stretch the bounds of the reader's credulity. ❜

Names can change depending on the relationship a character has with other characters. A character could be called:

◆ Elizabeth by her parents;

◆ Lizzie to her co-workers;

◆ Bet or Betty with friends and lovers.

This is true for a variety of names. Consider the types of character suggested by the different use of names with these pairings:

- Gerrard and Gez;

- Constantine and Connie;

- Theodore and Ted;

- Barbara and Babs.

The formality of the situation, and the relationship the character shares with other characters, will always dictate the name they are given in that context.

EXERCISE

Return to the list of names you created in the previous exercise. Re-read the names and reflect on the type of person each name suggests. Add to the list if you're unhappy with any of the choices. Add nicknames or contractions in the same fashion that Portnoy has used nicknames to identify her characters at the start of this chapter.

Select two names from the list for characters who you think could prove exciting characters in your fiction. We will start developing these characters in the next section.

WHAT DO YOUR CHARACTERS DESIRE?

Credible, interesting characters are invested with desire. All the obstacles that prevent a character from satisfying that desire are the conflicts that fuel the story.

- Anastasia, in *Fifty Shades of Grey*, desired Christian;

- Severin, in *Venus in Furs*, desired Wanda;

- Juliet, in Shakespeare's play, desired Romeo;

- Justine, in de Sade's story of the same name, desired piety;

◆ O, from Réage's novel *The Story of O*, desired to be of service to Master Steven.

Desire in relation to a fictional character does not always mean physical or sexual yearning for another person. Desire is an essential element of fully rounded characters in all fiction. But it doesn't have to be desire in the sense of lust or sexual need. Desire, in fiction, can be something as simple and universal as the need for a meal or the search for security. In erotic fiction it would be easy to use desire as a springboard for the story's sexual content. The danger with this approach is that it can be perceived as being too easy.

◆ Fiction centres on the resolution to questions raised early on in the story.

◆ Fiction allows us to see ingenious solutions to difficult and challenging problems.

◆ Fiction should never be about simple solutions to unchallenging problems.

❛ The editor of a successful UK erotic magazine issued a ban on stories that began in the style of: *"My name is Mandy and I love to suck guys . . ."*

Admittedly, this sort of opening does introduce the central character and her core desire but it offers no challenge to make the narrative interesting or intriguing. No reader is going to get through those first ten words and think, *"I wonder what's going to happen in this story?"* ❜

Demonstrating your characters' desires

In this short extract from the opening of a Nikki Magennis short story, 'The Red Shoes (Redux)', the heroine's core desire is fairly transparent:

The window stretched high above her head, the plate glass polished so bright it reflected her image like a mirror. But Lily wasn't looking at herself. Her gaze was totally transfixed on the shoes. Glossy, cherry-red, skyscraper high, patent-leather fuck-me shoes that made her heart beat faster just looking at them. They had deep curves and a dangerous heel and they stood centre stage on a podium by themselves, proud, shockingly beautiful and insanely unaffordable. They made Lily's mouth water. She could almost taste the red of them.

Magennis, N., 'The Red Shoes (Redux)'

This description takes place on the first page of the story and shows Lily's core desire. She wants to own a pair of red shoes. Specifically, she wants to own this particular pair of shoes, displayed in the shop window.

The description is a feast of sexual imagery. The shoes are described as:

♦ *glossy*;

♦ *cherry-red*; and

♦ *dangerous.*

Lily's response to them mimics the symptoms of sexual arousal.

♦ '*. . . her heart beat faster . . .*'

♦ '*They made Lily's mouth water.*'

♦ She considers the shoes as '*shockingly beautiful*'.

Magennis never lets us doubt that these shoes are wholly desirable. The description also shows us the conflict thwarting the immediate gratification of Lily's desire. The shoes are described as '*insanely unaffordable*'. Lily doesn't have the money for the shoes so the reader begins to wonder how she is going to pursue her goal of attaining them.

> ❛ Being unable to afford the shoes is a simple but effective conflict. Every reader at some point has experienced the frustration of not being able to afford something they desired. It's a familiar challenge universally faced by all of us. This makes Lily's predicament more engaging and allows the reader to empathise with her plight. ❜

I read this story and, on a subconscious level, I think: *Lily wants those shoes and she can't afford them. There are things I want but I can't afford – she's just like me.*

◆ Will Lily approach the shop owner and offer sex in exchange for the shoes? This is erotic fiction so that solution is not beyond the realms of possibility.

◆ Is Lily going to find some other sexual method of getting the money together? The story is in its earliest stages and the realms of possibility are wide open.

Whatever develops beyond these opening lines, the reader is already aware of Lily's defining desire and is empathising with her situation.

The same techniques can be seen below in the opening lines from Sommer Marsden's short story, 'The Student.'

'And here is the Wolff home,' he says. 'Even the most seasoned paranormal investigators will not go here.'

The house is a nightmare behind a chain-link fence, imposing and dark and falling apart.

'Why?' I don't get it. Why would this big-ass spooky mansion be off limits to ghost heads like us, the student body of NAPS? The North American Paranormal Society frowns on avoidance. I tap my pen and wait for our teacher to explain.

Marsden, S., 'The Student'

Again, we see the central character's core desire being fore-grounded in the opening of the story. The student, Helen Marsh, is a paranormal investigator. Her tutor tells her she is forbidden from entering '*this big-ass spooky mansion*' and Helen is clearly going to rebel.

As with the piece by Magennis, we can empathise with Marsden's central character. Each of us, at some point, has been told we are not allowed to do something. Even those of us who have not directly disobeyed such instructions have wondered what it would be like to rebel. Admittedly, Helen Marsh is being told she can't go into a haunted house, and most of us would be thankful for the refusal in those circumstances. But, even though most of us may have no urge to investigate a haunted house, we can identify with Helen's rebellious need to challenge authority.

- How will she achieve this?
- What will she have to do to get into the house?
- What will she encounter there?

All of these questions occur in the reader's mind because Marsden has presented us with a central character possessed by a very clear desire.

This is the core component for creating believable characters in fiction: invest them with an identifiable desire. Once the reader understands what the character wants, their interest in a well-written story will continue through to the final page where the desire should be satisfied.

EXERCISE

Take the two names you selected in the previous section and try to think what desires either of those characters might have. Do they want to own a particular pair of shoes? A car? Earn a promotion? Host the perfect dinner party? Win a sporting challenge? Are they keen to show their independence? Do they need to pass a test? Climb a mountain? Achieve something spectacular? Or do they simply want to claim the final thimble that will complete their collection?

Go back to the examples in this section. Notice how Magennis draws a detailed picture of the shoes and Lily's wanton sexual response to them. Notice how Marsden shows her character's impatience as she demands 'Why?' and counterpoints this question with an impatient tapping of her pen as she waits for her tutor's response. Neither of these pieces explicitly says: this is the character's desire. Yet, in both of them, we come away knowing what the character wants and we are sufficiently intrigued to read on and find out whether or not they achieve their goals.

Write about the desire your character has. Write about the object of the character's desire and make your reader understand why they are driven by that desire. Show your character's desires without the narrator needing to explain them explicitly to the reader.

CREATING CONFLICTS FOR YOUR CHARACTERS

Identifying a character's central desire allows us to see what conflicts and challenges they could face in the story. To be engaging and compelling, every story needs conflict.

In Mitzi Szereto's version of *Rapunzel*, the husband/father of the story tries to please his wife by scrumping an alligator-pear from their neighbour's garden. The desire here seems relatively simple:

♦ The wife/mother wants an alligator-pear.

♦ The husband/father wants to satisfy his wife's desire.

But the husband is caught in the act of stealing the alligator-pear and faces severe recriminations.

Weeping with relief, the grateful husband thanked his gap-toothed capturer and proceeded to shift himself back in the direction of home.

'On one condition,' added Old Gothel in an ominous tone.

The alligator-pear thief froze, dreading what would be coming next. Indeed, it was not considered prudent to strike a bargain with a witch, especially this *witch.*

'Ye must bestow unto me the child that shall be born of your wife.'

Szereto, M., 'Rapunzel'

Here we can see how the desire has caused escalating conflict.

- The husband and wife desired a child.
  - ◇ That desire was conflicted by fertility issues.

- To compensate for the lack of children in her relationship the wife transferred her desires onto food.
  - ◇ Consequently, it came as no surprise to the reader when she then desired an alligator-pear.

- To satisfy his wife's desires the husband agreed to steal this forbidden fruit from a dangerous neighbour.
  - ◇ To stop himself from being punished by the witch (because he desires to be unpunished) the husband agrees to the witch's sinister condition.

The story is building quickly and it's driven solely by desires and the conflicts that challenge those desires. This relationship between desires and conflicts is what fuels all fiction. It's richly exploited in the production of erotic fiction and sex scenes.

Conflicted desires don't need to be particularly complex. As I'm writing this, I desire a bar of chocolate. In itself, this wouldn't make an interesting story because there is no conflict. I could simply reach into my desk drawer, remove a bar of chocolate, and eat it. However, if I thought this desire would make an interesting story, I could set up challenges for the character wanting the chocolate.

- What if there was no chocolate in the house?

That's not a particularly demanding challenge. The character I'd originally envisioned lives in a contemporary town, no more than a five-minute walk away from a 24-hour shop. But it doesn't take much imagination to make these challenges sound more compelling.

- What if the nearest shop selling chocolate was a hundred miles away?

- What if there was some barrier between my character and the shop?

- What if the nearest shop selling chocolate was on a different planet?

Now the conflict challenging the central character's desire starts to look like a challenge worth reading about. Admittedly, it would be difficult to justify a long-distance journey (or an interstellar flight) solely for the sake of a bar of chocolate. But, in fiction, nothing is beyond the realm of possibility.

♦ What if the character desiring chocolate was on a diet? Now the situation takes on another aspect. We have an internalised conflict with a character wanting something and not wanting that same thing at the same time.

❛ Psychologists refer to this state of internalised conflict as *cognitive dissonance*. It's a mindset that can be seen in smokers and other addicts: wanting to indulge in a drug that at the same time they don't want to take because they know it's harmful to their health. Cognitive dissonance is indicative of levels of indecision that can work particularly well in BDSM fiction as the central character tries to balance their desire for sexual submission with their knowledge that the experience might be more extreme than they can tolerate. ❜

Returning to the example of the chocolate bar:

♦ How long has the character been dieting?

♦ Would a single chocolate bar matter in the great scheme of things?

♦ Would a single chocolate bar simply be the beginning of a binge of overindulgence?

♦ Could a chocolate bar lead to something else?

The character has two desires: to eat chocolate and to not eat chocolate.

♦ Which of those desires will triumph?

♦ What if there's chocolate in the house but getting it presents ethical problems?

There could be a box of chocolates, gift-wrapped and waiting for our central character's partner.

♦ Would the central character open that gift?

♦ Could the central character steal the chocolates?

♦ If they committed themselves to such a theft, would they try and cover their tracks or would they admit to the moment's weakness?

♦ Would there be repercussions?

There are other points to consider too:

♦ Does our central character keep their chocoholic status secret?

♦ Is it a secret that they share with an illicit friend?

♦ What other things are they likely to share with that illicit friend?

♦ How does this relationship conflict with the central character's morality?

❛ What started as sharing a discreet bar of chocolate with a chocolate buddy could escalate into a torrid affair based on sensual indulgence, deception and denial. The bar of chocolate here has become a metaphor for infidelity and it's analogous to gateway drugs, substance abuse and chemical dependence. ❜

Conflicts arise from character desire. Conflicts make our fiction interesting. Easily resolved conflicts are less intriguing. No one really wants to read about a character taking a five-minute walk to the local shop. But the more challenging conflicts can turn a commonplace need into something profound.

♦ Should the dieter eat the bar of chocolate?

♦ Which is preferable:
  ◊ the fulfilment of long-term goals or
  ◊ the satisfaction of immediate gratification?

♦ Is it justifiable to unwrap someone else's gift?

◆ What other trust issues could such an action uncover?

◆ Having a secret chocolate buddy may seem innocent – but doesn't secrecy always have a price?

EXERCISE

You already have names for two characters and a list of potential desires. Now select one of those desires and write about the conflict that prevents the character from achieving his or her desire.

Consider sexualising the desire.

Note the way Magennis has described the red shoes with the admiration of a lustful lover. Note that Magennis's central character responds to the source of her desire in a way that mimics sexual stimulation. Try to incorporate this level of heightened eroticism into your writing.

DESCRIBING YOUR CHARACTERS

He was a Red Sox fan.

I narrowed my eyes at him with a half-serious malevolence. He hadn't seen me yet. At that moment, he turned my way, and his face lit up when his eyes met mine. Then they dropped slightly to my jacket.

I was wearing my Yankees pullover, and his expression immediately shifted to one of surprise – and then to a challenging gaze similar to mine. We were both aware, I was sure, that our respective teams would be facing off that very night with the first of a three-game series against each other in New York. Still standing a good twenty yards away from him, I lifted my head and I looked him up and down. Then I stared hard at him, holding back a smile. Even as I felt the heat rising in me, I tossed my head and turned on my heel. I felt him watching my ass as I walked haughtily back in the direction from which I had come.

A Red Sox fan. Unbelievable.

My team had better win tonight, I told myself.

Emerald, 'Who's on Top?'

In this passage Emerald shows us two characters about to go into direct conflict. They support opposing teams that are about to face one another in an important game. The conflict is inevitable. Corey is wearing a cap with a red letter B on the brim: the logo of the Boston Red Sox. Paige is wearing a pullover emblazoned with the design of the New York Yankees. We know nothing about the individuals except that they're both committed sports fans and whatever relationship had been blossoming between them is now about to be tested by this conflict.

There are four ways to describe a character.

- Appearance;

- Speech;

- Action;

- Thought.

Each of these elements contributes to the reader's understanding of the character's personality. The way each of these is presented will depend on point of view, relevance to the story and how the author wants the character to be seen.

Appearance refers to a character's clothes, her or his facial expressions, body language, and their reaction to situations and other characters. Each of these areas says something about the character being described.

Speech is also distinctive to each character. What is said, and how it is said, can speak volumes about the person saying those words.

Actions show how a character responds to a situation and can sometimes tell the reader more than dialogue or a sentence detailing the motives for a character's deeds.

Having access to a character's **thoughts** can give us an insight into the reasoning behind a specific choice of appearance, speech or action: giving the reader a better understanding of the personality involved.

Any of these in isolation can create an interesting character. Combined, these modes of description can bring life to the characters we create.

Appearance

Opposite me by the massive Renaissance fireplace sat Venus; she was not a casual woman of the half-world, who under this pseudonym wages war against the enemy sex, like Mademoiselle Cleopatra, but the real, true goddess of love.

She sat in an armchair and had kindled a crackling fire, whose reflection ran in red flames over her pale face with its white eyes, and from time to time over her feet when she sought to warm them.

Her head was wonderful in spite of the dead stony eyes; it was all I could see of her. She had wrapped her marble-like body in a huge fur, and rolled herself up trembling like a cat.

Sacher-Masoch, L., 'Venus in Furs'

In this description we see Sacher-Masoch's description of Venus. This is an unusual piece of writing in that the woman being described would defy what is conventionally thought of as being attractive.

- Venus is shown to have a pale face with white eyes.
- Her head possesses *dead stony eyes* and her body is *marble-like.*
- The only warmth in the character is that being reflected from the fire where she sits.

Ordinarily we would say that this style of description slows down the pace of a narrative. However, these paragraphs give us an insight into the way Venus is being appraised and the mindset of the man admiring her. Her attributes of being cold and marble-like are seen, by the narrator, as desirable traits. This tells us as much about his fetishes as they say about Venus's physical appearance.

❝ Appearance is possibly the most obvious method of describing a character. Physical description gives us an idea of what a person looks like. Brunette, redhead, blonde? Tall, broad, fat or thin? Flat-chested, buxom, athletic or willowy? These are essential details that need to be conveyed so the reader has a fuller understanding of the characters in your fiction. But how does a writer convey these details without slowing down the pace of the story? ❞

The following example is from a more contemporary erotic short story.

The Director of Finance. Stone. Mr Stone. Clever Bobby. Whatever.

Well, he's a tall man, and imposing. Not fat exactly but no Greek god either. Just an average-looking, middle-aged, slightly grey-ing, five o'clock shadowy (he says he has Italian ancestry), suit-wearing local government bigwig.

Theoretically he's the sort of bloke you wouldn't look twice at in a crowd, especially if there was plenty of younger talent around. But in practice well, he makes my knees disintegrate and this yearning, gnawing sensation start up somewhere around where I think my heart is.

I'm just about to topple over when, thank Christ, he says, 'Take a seat, Maria.'

Da Costa, P., *Entertaining Mr Stone*

In this passage Da Costa's narrator is clearly enamoured of Mr Stone. We get descriptions of him that show that his appearance is average.

◆ He wears a suit.

◆ He has a five o'clock shadow.

◆ He's *not fat exactly*, which means he's probably *not thin exactly* either.

He's a man whom the reader can see as being remarkable only because he's unremarkable. And, despite this unremarkable appearance, he's an obvious focus for the narrator's desire.

❛ Describing characters can be a two-way process. The more the narrator tells us about a character, the more we get to understand her and her desires. In this passage, notice how Maria says she gets a *yearning, gnawing sensation* around the place where she thinks her *heart is*. Aside from having effectively described Bobby Stone, doesn't this final note suggest Maria is a character who is trying to resist the idea of being in love? ❜

Looking at her, his thoughts veered from professional to personal. Tall and slim, she wore a tight, red dress, clinging to every lush curve and perfectly matching her bright stiletto fuck-me pumps. No longer tied up with the scarf matching her outfit, her black hair cascaded around her shoulders like the spread of a raven's wings.

Quinn, D., *Flesh and the Devil*

This example shows a male protagonist admiring a female sex worker he has employed for the evening. Again, with this being erotic fiction, the description is sexualised.

- The red dress clings *to every lush curve.*

- Her footwear is described as *fuck-me pumps.*

- *. . . black hair cascaded around her shoulders like the spread of a raven's wings.*

Readers come to erotic fiction for sexual stimulation and Quinn is providing the readers with what they want.

But we should also notice here how much action is going on in this simple piece of description. The red dress is *clinging* to every lush curve. The red dress is *matching* her pumps. Her black hair has *cascaded* around her shoulders. Aware that the pace of the story is essential for maintaining reader interest, Quinn does not keep the description static.

She describes the woman as *tall and slim,* and the style of the dress is simply referred to as *tight.* The pace of the narrative doesn't slow while Quinn explains the details of the hemline, any appliqué work on the décolletage, or the double-stitching at the sides of the concealed zipper at the back. Here Quinn is showing us only those details the central character observes: all the details that the reader needs to know to get sufficient description of this character's appearance before moving on to the important aspects of the story's events.

❛ It's worth noting here that appearance needs to be consistent. When creating a character it's advisable to make detailed notes about their appearance so that future descriptions remain consistent. Hair and eye-colour are notorious features that can change due to an author's lapse in concentration. Body shape needs to be decided early on and maintained consistently throughout the story.   ❜

Looking good naked

In erotic fiction it's imperative for the author to know his or her characters on the most intimate level. What does each character look like naked?

◆ How big are her breasts?

◆ Is she happy with the shape and size?

◆ Does she wish they were bigger? Smaller?

◆ Is s/he comfortable being naked?

◆ Is he oversized or undersized?

◆ How does each character deal with pubic hair?
  ◇ Is it an unmaintained clump of curls?
  ◇ Is it shaved neatly into a heart shape?
  ◇ Or does s/he frequently visit a salon for a full Brazilian as well as anal bleaching?

Be aware of how each character looks naked, and understand how comfortable they are with their personal nudity. Knowing these details and keeping them consistent through your story will create believable characters for your erotic fiction.

❛ There's a common myth associated with erotic fiction that every character needs to be attractive. To some degree this is true. The central characters in all fiction need to be perceived as attractive for readers to have an interest in their story. But physical attractiveness is not the whole story.   ❜

Physical attractiveness is subjective. For every person drawn to the muscular physique of a bodybuilder, there is someone equally repulsed by that body type. For everyone drawn to the androgynous appeal of a supermodel, there is someone else complaining about the lack of curves in a size zero. Arguably, attractiveness is more about personality than appearance and we shall look at that aspect in the following sections.

EXERCISE

Outline a brief physical description of the characters you have been creating. Use the examples from above as templates and sexualise the descriptions. Try to use the techniques that Quinn has employed and make the description active rather than static.

You might want to show one character describing another, so that the reader has an opportunity to see what the describer perceives as attractive qualities.

Consider the way Sacher-Masoch sexualises Venus's coldness and stony qualities. Is there something distinctive about one of your characters that another character would find singularly attractive?

Consider the way Portia Da Costa shows her narrator admiring the unremarkable Mr Stone. Can your narrator admire someone who does not have many admirable qualities?

Try describing a single detail about a character: the colour of her lipstick, the shadow of his razor stubble, the shapeliness of her legs or the tightness of his backside.

Speech

'You're wanking over my comic,' she screeched, lashing out at him. 'You fucking wanker'!

'I'm not hurting it.' He crossed his arms in front of his face to ward her off.

'You're disgusting.'

*'You're the one who buys this stuff. I don't suppose you get it just
to admire the artistry. And it certainly isn't for the story.'*

Ellis, M., *Dark Designs*

This is the opening exchange between the male and female
leads in Madelynne Elis's novel, *Dark Designs.*

◆ Notice how both characters are comfortable using taboo
language.

◆ Notice how they easily intellectualise sex and sexuality
without making the exchange sound contrived or gratuitous.

◆ Notice how their animosity is laying the seeds of conflict for
a romantic relationship.

❛ There is a full chapter on dialogue later in the book. However,
for this section, it's essential to understand the importance of
speech and how what is said can define a character.   ❜

The characters here, even if they weren't discussing Yaoi comic
books, would be instantly identifiable as being young and
British.

◆ They use the modern swear words of young British characters.

◆ They show their dislike for each other with easily expressed
contempt.

◆ They speak quickly without seeming to think if their words
are too harsh.

It's effective dialogue that introduces the characters and their
relationship as they first meet. If any of your characters had to
interact like these two, would they use exactly the same words,
or would their lines need rephrasing?

Consider any of the characters you've been creating and answer
the following questions:

◆ How does you character say hello?

Hi! Howdy! Bonjour! Good morning!

The level of formality used in any greeting will always differ depending on who a character is addressing. Think about the different personalities suggested by two characters when one says, 'Good morrow,' and the other replies with, 'Wassup?' Between them they've only exchanged three words, yet already we know a lot about both speakers.

◆ Does your character use a chat-up line?
  ◇ *What's a nice guy/girl like you doing in a place like this?*
  ◇ *If I could rearrange the alphabet I'd put U and I next to each other.*
  ◇ *Is that a gun in your pocket, or are you just pleased to see me?*
  ◇ *Did it hurt when you fell from heaven?*

Each one of these could be perceived as a cheesy line that should only be appropriate for a cheesy character. But each one could also be delivered with irony in a role-playing session between partners with an established sexual connection. Chat-up lines are only ever icebreakers and they can carry negative associations. Do your characters avoid them? Do your characters use them effectively? Or do some of your characters dismiss them for fear of being perceived as shallow?

❛ The danger with chat-up lines is that they can come across as clichés. More importantly, for anyone writing erotica, a chat-up line should not be used as an infallible talisman for luring a partner into their clutches. The myth of the surefire chat-up line is a teenage fable that has no place in contemporary erotic fiction. ❜

◆ Which rude words do your characters use?
  ◇ Does he look at her breasts and think of them as: *tits, boobies* or *melons?*
  ◇ Does she refer to a penis as his thing? His wing-wang? Or his love-truncheon?

◇ Do your characters refer to sex acts as *shagging, bonking,* or *doing the nasty?*

None of these options suggests great levels of sexual maturity but few characters (fictional or otherwise) use biological definitions all the time.

Moreover, it can be seen that a female character who refers to her own genitals as 'my personal pleasure palace' has a different attitude towards sex from a character who uses the phrase 'my dirty bits'. Similarly, a male character who refers to a penis as his 'thingy' has a different opinion of sex from the man who talks about his 'beefy broadsword'.

❝ In erotic fiction the writer will need to know each character's sexual vocabulary. It's prudent to consider any specific labels a character uses for genitalia, intercourse, the opposite sex and unconventional sexual practices. ❞

Every word a character says is going to reveal more about them than the content of what is being said. Always make sure each character's speech is appropriate for their personality and the situation in which they are involved.

EXERCISE

Write down your character's main ways of greeting the following people:

◆ a same-sex friend;

◆ a subordinate colleague;

◆ a superior colleague;

◆ a potential sexual partner.

Write down your character's typical response to an unwanted event. Do they say: 'Fudge!', 'Damnation!' or 'Fiddlesticks!'? Do they shrug, say nothing, and flash a resigned smile in the face of adversity? Or do they turn to the person standing next to them and start to transfer the blame? Notice how each of these responses suggests a different type of personality.

What does your character say during sex? Do they murmur approving and encouraging comments? Do they issue instructions and directions, explaining what they like and what they don't like? Or do they simply grunt, squeal and exclaim until the whole ordeal is concluded? Again, notice how this is revealing more about the speaker than the words that are being said.

Actions

One day, about the middle of November, I was with my brother François, two years younger than I, in my father's room, watching him attentively as he was working at optics. A large lump of crystal, round and cut into facets, attracted my attention. I took it up, and having brought it near my eyes I was delighted to see that it multiplied objects. The wish to possess myself of it at once got hold of me, and seeing myself unobserved I took my opportunity and hid it in my pocket.

A few minutes after this my father looked about for his crystal, and unable to find it, he concluded that one of us must have taken it. My brother asserted that he had not touched it, and I, although guilty, said the same; but my father, satisfied that he could not be mistaken, threatened to search us and to thrash the one who had told him a story. I pretended to look for the crystal in every corner of the room, and, watching my opportunity I slyly slipped it in the pocket of my brother's jacket. At first I was sorry for what I had done, for I might as well have feigned to find the crystal somewhere about the room; but the evil deed was past recall. My father, seeing that we were looking in vain, lost patience, searched us, found the unlucky ball of crystal in the pocket of the innocent boy, and inflicted upon him the promised thrashing.

Casanova, J., *The Memoirs of Casanova*

Actions speak louder than words. In this passage from Casanova's memoirs, we get a glimpse of the main character's entire personality from his actions.

- He explains his desire for an object that is multifaceted and pretty.
- He shows us his fear of consequences and repercussions.
- He shows us that he has a duplicitous nature.

Even for anyone unfamiliar with Casanova's work, and only aware of his reputation as a promiscuous libertine, this passage gives us a glimpse of the man that this boy is destined to become. This is a perfect illustration of the adage that writers should 'show not tell.' We are shown what Casanova is like through his actions, not simply told he is capable of unconscionable behaviour.

> Actions are an incredibly useful way of presenting a character to a reader. Combined with descriptions of appearance, thought and speech they can help writers to create full, rounded and credible characters.

It's her music, the plaintive strains of Light my Fire. *The curtains glide open and the spotlight falls on her as she sways her way to the front of the audience. She looks dignified in a long black feathered evening gown that makes a little sound as she walks. It shimmies its way right down to her calves. Her breasts and hips move in unison, two halves of a perfect whole. Her hair is fashionably raven, swept back in a glossy parting over her face to fall in perfect waves down to her shoulders. It's worn as if it was a diamond necklace. There's something doll-like about her glamour, her cheeks un-rouged. The paleness only accentuates her perfectly made-up eyes, the stained red lips. Every ounce of her speaks desire. When she moves, it's controlled. If she was kissed, surely it wouldn't dent her lip-line. Fi-EEERRR! She turns away from the audience. A coy flick of her hair and her gown drops. From somewhere to the left there is a murmur of approval.*

Perks, M., 'The Performing Breasts'

In this story from Marcelle Perks, we're presented with a character who works as a burlesque dancer. Consequently Perks takes full advantage of this role and shows us the character in the act of dancing.

In some ways this description is only telling us about Lydia's appearance. We get to see what she's wearing, what her make-up looks like and the doll-like aspect of her features. But throughout the piece Lydia is dancing:

◆ She shimmies.

◆ She sways.

◆ Her breasts and hips move in perfect unison.

All of these actions show the dancer dancing. With the final two sentences from this passage, when Lydia drops her gown, we can almost sympathise with the murmur of approval she hears from the audience.

EXERCISE

You've already created a character, given them a name, described aspects of their appearance and put words in their mouth. Now show them in action. Write a short scene where your character is involved with someone else. There doesn't need to be any dialogue.

What can your character say without speaking? Does he shrug? Raise an eyebrow? Does she pass a beguiling smile? Blow a kiss? It's already been noted that actions speak louder than words: Does he steal a kiss? Does she give him a glimpse of bare shoulder?

Thoughts

Lori stared at the total in her electronic shopping cart and winced – $323.79. Who knew sexual experimentation was so darned expensive? She debated which of the various items she could delete. The nipple clamps? No . . . Kent had mentioned those on several occasions.

What about the swimsuit-style body wear made of black feathers? It was pretty expensive. And it might make her look like a black Donald Duck. But no . . . she had a hankering to see Kent's face when she stroked him with her feathers.

She sighed. There really wasn't a single thing on the list that she was willing to part with. She moved the cursor over the PLACE ORDER button, closed her eyes, and clicked.

Scott, E., *Naughty Housewives*

Depending on the viewpoint used, thought can bring a character to life in a more convincing way than any other medium. In this example we see Lori's thoughts as she makes an online purchase.

◆ We can see her debating whether or not to keep certain items.

◆ We can understand how she validates each decision.

◆ We are given a huge insight into the sort of person she is and the relationship she shares with Kent.

❛ When watching films and TV shows we can see and hear what characters are doing and how they are interacting. We can see their actions and appearance and we can hear their dialogue. However, with the exception of narrated off-screen dialogue and monologues, we have no access to what's going on inside the character's mind. Written fiction, novels and short stories, are able to give us an insight into what a character is thinking. This allows for a greater intimacy between the reader and the characters and a better understanding of their personality. ❜

Consider the following passage:

I'd been counting off the days, and boy, had they ever dragged. But I figured that if I could get to the end of the first week, I could maybe make it to week two.

Maybe.

I just had to prove I could last through my one-month contract. Biting the bullet and taking an office job had been the absolute pits in the first place, but I couldn't drift from college course to college course any longer. The time had come to quell my rebellious streak, tame my multicoloured mop, take out my nose ring and don an acceptably smart outfit. What a crime, *I thought to myself, when I'd packed away my usual, much more alternative wardrobe, and headed for the temp agency.*

Walker, S., 'TGIF'

In this example we have immediate access to the first-person narrator's thoughts.

◆ We understand that the days have been dragging in her new job.

◆ She is a former college student and rebel.

◆ She is trying to come to terms with the minutiae of office life.

◆ There is also a subtext here where we understand that this change has been made through necessity rather than on a whim.

I couldn't drift from college course to college course any longer. The time had come to quell my rebellious streak . . .

Walker never says why this character needs to make such sweeping changes in her life because these details aren't important to the story.

◆ Have the character's parents thrown her out of the house, or threatened her with eviction if she doesn't find a job?

It's a possibility but, even if that was the case, it would be unnecessary information for the purposes of this short story.

◆ Has the character grown tired of the feckless existence of being a student?

It's another possibility but, again, the presentation of this information would detract from the intentions of Walker's narrative.

❝ Thoughts are best treated as unspoken dialogue. Psychologists are still unsure as to whether or not we think in words and sentences or images and concepts. Rather than trying to express thought exactly as it occurs in the human mind, readers will more easily be able to understand a text where thoughts are shown as unsaid words. ❞

Because Walker's story is about how the central character deals with the changes of moving from the status of college student to office worker, it's enough for us to know she is resolved to make that change. We can be entertained by the way she goes on to marry the two concepts of being a rebel and being an office worker as the story develops.

This all could have been conveyed through other means but no alternative would have been quite as effective. If there had been a scene where we saw this character washing the colour out of her hair and removing her nose ring before applying for the job, we might have seen what she was doing. But the pace would have slowed considerably. If Walker had begun the narrative with dialogue, where the central character was explaining her current predicament to someone, it would have meant the introduction of a redundant character. Instead, because this story opens with the character's thoughts being laid bare to the reader, we enter the story knowing that she has an overwhelming desire to make this new job work.

EXERCISE

Take your writing from the previous section on **Actions** and write a follow-up scene for the next day.

In physics we are told that, for every action, there is an equal and opposite reaction. The same is true in fiction.

- How does your character feel about the events that occurred?
- Does she or he regret what happened?
- Is she or he planning a repeat performance?

Write down the central character's thoughts as they reflect on the scene.

SUMMARY

Well-crafted, identifiable and sympathetic characters will bring your fiction to life. Once the reader is able to understand and empathise with your characters they will be committed to the story being told and eager to find out more.

- Characters are the most important aspect of fiction.
- Names are as important in fiction as they are in real life.
- Develop your characters with care.

Characters in fiction are driven by desires.

- Give your characters desires with which readers can sympathise:
  ◇ this causes empathy.
- Give your characters desires that are not easily satisfied:
  ◇ this causes conflict.

Keep detailed notes about your characters and remain consistent to these details throughout your narrative. Describe characters through:

- physical appearance;
- speech;
- actions;
- thoughts.

Keep in mind the adage of 'Show: don't tell.' Trust the reader to see and understand how and why the character has reacted in a specific way.

5 *Planning a compelling plot*

GETTING TO GRIPS WITH PLOTS AND OUTLINES

Plotting is not popular among some writers. They argue that:

- The mechanics of plotting are not really creative.

- Working to the templates of predefined outlines is not being creative.

- Writing within the parameters of what has previously worked for other writers and readers is not really being creative.

But it has to be acknowledged that the idea of using tried-and-tested methods for telling a convincing story is a useful facility for any writer to have at their disposal.

One of the criticisms often levelled at plotting is that it spoils the personal level of intrigue some writers need in order to maintain interest in a project. Once a writer knows how a story will develop, he or she no longer has any interest in working on the story. The action of writing down an outline (rather than writing the story itself) destroys the writer's enthusiasm for the project.

This is a fair criticism for some. We all approach writing differently and it's likely true for many writers. However, for those who are able to plot, the discipline of outlining a story can offer many rewards.

EXERCISE

Consider the climactic scene of a story you want to write. Your two characters have finally got together after overcoming so many hurdles and they get to fulfil their fantasies in each other's arms.

Write this final scene in 500 words or less.

Now that you have this scene complete, try to decide what would happen next if this were the *opening* scene for your story. Are you able to see a way for this story to continue? Would this new story be stronger or weaker than your original idea? If you can't see a way for the story to continue, how would you write the opening to this story now you know how it's going to finish? Do you still have the same enthusiasm for this story now you know how it's going to end?

Try to develop an outline for your story with this scene as either the beginning or the conclusion.

There have been lots of pages written about plots. Various authors have tried to identify the limited number of plots:

◆ 36: Georges Polti, *36 Dramatic Situations*;

◆ 20: Ronald Tobias, *20 Master Plots*;

◆ seven: *The Seven Basic Plots*, Christopher Booker;

◆ three: *The Basic Patterns of Plot*, William Foster-Harris;

◆ two: the suggestion that all Hollywood films can be broken down into stories about 'someone leaving home' or stories about 'a stranger coming to town';

◆ one: Joseph Campbell's monomyth, *The Hero with a Thousand Faces*.

While this is a fascinating area of study it's too broad to be considered here with any depth. Also, for the majority of writers, the only practical value this information gives is that we shouldn't worry about a perceived lack of originality in the structure of our storytelling because every story has been told before. However, it's worth reflecting on the following archetypes:

◆ A romance will typically be a story of two characters meeting, overcoming obstacles, and finally getting together (or not).

◆ A horror story will typically show a hero discovering, battling and then vanquishing a monster.

◆ A western most often shows a single good man bringing order and justice to a scene of chaos and anarchy.

Because these stories have a similar shape this does not mean that they are unoriginal. It only means that there is a typical structure that supports stories within these genres. *Wuthering Heights*, *Pride and Prejudice* and *Fifty Shades of Grey* could all be perceived as following the typical outline for a romance – yet we're all aware that the three stories are drastically different from each other.

EXERCISE

Reflect on three of your favourite novels. They don't have to be erotica.

◆ Do these stories share any similarities with each other?

◆ Do they have any similarities with any other stories you know?

◆ Are any of these stories completely original and totally unlike any other story you've ever read?

Try to compile a list of stories that you think are based on the same plot structure. Make notes to explain why you think they're similar.

BREAKING DOWN A BASIC STRUCTURE

Aristotle identified that fiction is made up of a beginning, a middle and an end. While this comes across as a simplistic way of breaking down a story, it's a useful reminder of what needs to go where.

- **In the beginning**

  Here we introduce the important characters and the basic conflict they are going to face throughout the remainder of the story. Beginnings are of vital importance to writers and readers, grabbing interest and setting the tone for what's to come.

- **In the middle**

  The characters go through the escalating process of encountering conflicts and trying to resolve their difficulties.

- **In the end**

  Having resolved the conflict, or having learnt to live with an unresolved conflict, the story concludes.

❝ The conclusion to a story is as important as the beginning or the middle. Mickey Spillane, the successful crime writer, said, "The first page sells the book. The last page sells the next book." He's right to point out that the last part of the story is what a reader will remember when they're looking for the next novel they want to enjoy. Over the next few pages we're going to consider each of these various elements in greater detail. ❞

In the beginning

Character and situation

There are several ways of starting a story. One of the most straightforward is to simply begin by introducing the central character and their situation. It's an expository style of storytelling that doesn't suit everyone but it is an efficient way of getting the reader to understand what's happening within the story world.

Seven years of her life gone, wasted.

But that wasn't exactly true. She had been doing a lot more with her time than just being in love with a person she never wants to see again. How these things happen is a mystery millions of men and women have pondered throughout the ages, yet Sofia always believed herself magically immune to such protracted catastrophes. She scarcely noticed the mileage accumulating, the years flowing by before the crash, when she suddenly realized the promising love she had wholeheartedly bought into had degenerated into a routine shell not worth fixing.

Pita, M. I., Moonlight's Edge

This expository opening gives us a detailed overview of Sofia's situation at the start of the story.

◆ It's clear from this passage that Sofia is intent on making a new start.

◆ It's obvious that this new start will form the basis of the story we're about to read.

◆ In short, this is an effective introduction to the story's central character and the change that affects her current situation.

Equally expository is Stan Kent's opening to his short story, 'Aisle Seat'.

I'd decided to burn up all the frequent-flyer miles that I'd accumulated over the years of jetting here and there and splurge on a business class seat to Rome for a long weekend in the Eternal City. After some frustrating ordeals dealing with airline websites and operators protected from human contact by a maze of phone options, I was able to score a seat on an Alitalia 747 from Los Angeles to Rome. The only problem was that I couldn't get a window seat. I don't like aisle seats because it never fails that just after I've fallen asleep the person next to me decides to go to the bathroom, and even in the relative spaciousness of business class, it still disturbs my hard-fought-for slumber, and then there's no way I can get back to sleep. I wind up staying up all night reading or writing or watching some movies I really don't want to watch.

Kent, S., 'Aisle Seat'

Kent's narrator explains a lot of things in this short passage:

◆ He explains how he has ended up on the plane.

◆ We know where he's going and how he's been able to afford it.

◆ The narrator gives us some details about the frustration of ordering airline tickets.

◆ He also mentions the nuisance of not being able to get the right seat.

However, while these openings are expository, and only appear to be telling us facts about each character's life and existence, they're also revealing important backstory that will become relevant later in the tale. As soon as these openings are concluded, the reader knows they will be comfortably immersed in a narrative where they understand the main characters and have a grasp of the situations that are likely to impact on them.

EXERCISE

Write a detailed introduction for a story that describes one character in a static situation.

◆ In Pita's story we see a character reflecting on a relationship that has ended.

◆ In Kent's story we see a character having gone through the preamble of booking an airline ticket.

Write your own expository scene where you describe events that lead to your character being in a specific situation or in a certain location. Aim to achieve this in no more than two or three short paragraphs.

Action

One of the most common methods of starting a story is *in medias res* – in the middle of things. The opening lines to any story are essential for grabbing and holding reader interest. Starting in the middle of an engaging, intriguing or erotic scene ensures the reader will be engrossed in events, making them want to read more to get to know the characters in your fiction.

This example comes from the Perks and Mullins short story, 'Underneath.'

They coughed between kisses, sucking in the mold-ridden air as sex-lust quickened their needs. The man leaned down to enter her mouth, his body mimicking the curve of the ceiling. His hand pushed and slid to part her as the metal gods roared their approval. In, tight and holding, both thrilled further by the vibrations of the tunnels around them. The searing singing! Ah, so good! Just a wall beyond there were people chatting about West End shows, something about Britney Spears. They were going home, easing the day away. But the real underground was here, where life was deadened. It was sealed disharmony, a jerking cock-in-the-mouth, a secret world where fugitives took a mystery trip to the unconscious.

Perks and Mullins, 'Underneath'

Immediately here, because Perks and Mullins have started this story in the middle of a sex scene, the reader should be compelled to continue. The sexual tension is made explicit in the opening line and it continues throughout this passage and into the remainder of the story. More than that, the authors of this passage have given the encounter an unusual twist in that their characters are having sex in an unusual location.

> ❦ *In medias res* is a common device that's used across genres but it's a particularly useful device in erotica. Some readers turn to erotic fiction looking solely for graphic descriptions of sex and intimacy. If the reader finds those erotic descriptions in the opening lines of the story, they're more likely to continue reading.

Not that the subject of an effective *in medias res* opening always needs to be sexual. This point is illustrated below in the start to Mathilde Madden's novella-length story, 'Under Her Skin'.

She's running down the corridor. She hasn't stopped running since the letter came this morning. Running, running, running, running on adrenaline.

She tried to go to the library. The one here and the one at her parents' house, but she was so damned jumpy that the words wouldn't lie still on the pages of each book she tried to read.

But that doesn't matter. She doesn't need to read up on vampires now. She's known about such monsters since before she could talk.

Madden, M., 'Under Her Skin'

Madden here introduces us to her central character, Merle, and shows us that Merle lives in a world of monstrous vampires. In this scene we see that Merle is nervous, jumpy and running to somewhere or from something. This might not be an opening that captures every reader's attention. Those with no interest in vampires will probably put this story aside. But by this early stage in the story, the rest of us should be anxious to know how Merle's story develops.

EXERCISE

Start with an engaging scene.

Don't worry about the characters involved or how they have arrived at this point. Put your central character(s) in a situation that you personally find compelling. Write the scene so that it draws the reader in. You can worry about backstory later.

Aim to write as many paragraphs as are needed to convey the sense of danger, excitement or sexual passion that are at the core of this scene.

The hook

One of the most popular methods of opening a story is the hook. The hook is a narrative device that:

◆ offers a compelling beginning;

◆ instantly captures the reader's attention;

◆ drags the reader into the story.

Consider the following example from Cheyenne Blue.

It started when I kidnapped her dog.

I didn't exactly tie him up and hold him for ransom. He simply preferred me – at least he did in the daytime when my neighbour, Karen was at work. He was a small black-and-tan terrier; the scruffy sort that is excellent company. He'd tactfully stay next door until Karen's car had disappeared down the driveway, then his ears would prick, and he'd wait for my call.

Blue, C., 'The Hairy Matchmaker'

The opening line here is a wonderful attention-grabber. Kidnapping any creature, human or animal, is harsh and unconscionable behaviour. However, before we decide that Blue's character is advocating such cruelty, the statement is revised and we read on. Before we know it, Blue has introduced two central characters (who are both animal-lovers), a dog and the potential conflict that will come when the terrier's ownership is inevitably called into question.

- ◆ It's an effective and concise opening to a story.
- ◆ It grabs the reader's attention.
- ◆ It makes us want to read on.

Megan Clark provides a more thoughtful (but no less effective) opening to her erotic novel, *Seduce Me*.

When a person speaks the name of a lover, much is revealed. Too much, because the tone of voice and the expression in the eyes as the name is spoken will lay bare the depth of that person's love. So that the name itself becomes an emblem of the person's vulnerability, of the degree to which that person's heart is exposed. Not another word need be said. The name is enough.

'Carissa,' he says, pointedly, as if to prove he remembers her name. He looks up at her, eyes hungry. His voice is strong, but devoid of affection, 'Oh, a goddess you are.'

Clark, M., *Seduce Me*

This is another attention-grabbing opening to a story. The narrator tells us that much can be revealed from the way a lover speaks a person's name. It's an insight that most of us will speculate might be applied to our own lives.

This passage also works on other levels.

We're told that much is revealed when a person speaks the name of a lover. And then, when Carissa's name is spoken by her lover, his voice is devoid of affection. It's an intelligent beginning to a story that encourages the reader to explore the layers of meaning being presented.

❛ *The key to writing an effective hook is to remember the acronym SIR. An effective hook should be:*

◆ *Short*

◆ *Intriguing*

◆ *Relevant*

If the opening lines are short, the reader is drawn in by the ease of the writing. If there is intrigue, the reader will want to know more. And, obviously, the passage needs to be relevant to the rest of the story. ❜

Kristina Lloyd is equally gifted at providing an attention-grabbing opener as she shows here in her delightful short story, 'All My Lovers in One Room'.

Yeah, that's right: all my lovers, past and present, and it's not a big room either. This could be a horror story, and maybe it is because I can't see the ending from here. There are thirty-seven men and two women, but even without counting, I know someone is missing.

Fancy him being late for my deathbed!
Lloyd, K., 'All My Lovers in One Room'

In this opening passage we are immediately intrigued by the un-usual situation of so many people being crowded into a room with one person – all of whom are cited as former lovers of the central character. It's an opening worthy of Kafka for its surreal quality.

◆ We're given a suggestion of promiscuity because there are 40 characters in the room including the first person narrator.

- There are echoes of sexual ambiguity because there are men and women in the room.

- Lloyd has immediately hooked the reader into wanting to read more in the quest to find out what is going on in this story.

EXERCISE

Hook your reader with an intriguing opening line. Think of some way to capture your reader's interest, either with an insightful observation in the style of Megan Clark's *Seduce Me*, or with an outrageous or puzzling remark such as those demonstrated by Cheyenne Blue and Kristina Lloyd.

Compare the results of this exercise with the previous one.

- Which opening did you prefer to write?

- Do you think both are equally valid?

- Does one way of writing an opening lend itself to a different type of story or a different style of character?

In the middle

Playing consequences

Plot, at its most basic level, can be seen as the relationship between action and reaction. A character, faced with a decision, makes a choice. The consequences of that choice (and the next one and the next one) are what make the story we find so compelling.

❛ Newton's third law of motion tells us that: for every action there is an equal and opposite reaction. This applies just as much to characters in fiction as it does to physics. Every time a character makes a decision, the consequences of that decision will impact on the character and help develop a compelling story. ❜

We can see the importance of choice and consequences in the following exchange between the exotic dancer, Brittany, and the narrator, Professor Marcum, in Michelle Houston's short story.

'I'll make you a deal, Professor.'

I arched an eyebrow at her, trying to mold my face in my stern look, knowing it failed miserably. Three margaritas tended to make me mellow. Since this was my career on the line, I would have thought my body would be a bit more cooperative. Knowing I wasn't going to be able to stare her down, I settled for waiting to hear her ultimatum. She had earned an A in my class.

'Dance with me, and I won't tell a soul that I saw you here tonight or any other night you care to come back.'

Houston, M., 'Tempted'

Brittany could have asked Professor Marcum to do many things. Her innocent request for a dance makes it deceptively easy for the narrator to acquiesce. But what will be the consequences of this action? The Professor is already in a compromising situation by this stage of the story. Will a dance help the character avoid further consequences? Or are there likely to be more repercussions?

'There's a tap on my back. It's Shirley. I have no fear now. 'Leave me alone!' I shout.

'Oh Debra, calm down! I'm sorry if I upset you.'

'I dropped my fucking keys, so just leave me alone! Please just leave me alone!'

'You dropped your keys?'

'Yes! Down the fucking shaft. I can't get into my house or my car now! Dave went to work, and to make matters worse, I left my phone at home.'

'I don't own a cell phone, but come with me. You can wait at my house until Dave can fetch you.'

'No! Dave will come get me here. I don't need any help from you!'

'Are you sure? It's awful cold out.'

'Yes!' I march back into the post office and then look in my purse for a quarter to use in their pay phone, but I don't have one. Shirley is still standing outside, staring at me though the window. Why won't she fucking leave? She motions for me to follow her to her car.

I have two choices: beg to use somebody's phone or get in Shirley's car. I choose Shirley's car. I don't know why. Maybe because it's so damned cold out.

Du Pré, J., 'Before the Move'

In this piece we can see that Debra has a choice: either ignore Shirley's offer of help or accept assistance from someone she despises. Debra is wedged firmly between a rock and a hard place. She doesn't want to be beholden to Shirley but she needs to get home. All her other options for an acceptable resolution to this problem have been whittled away by Du Pré's clever storytelling. And so she's left having to accept Shirley's invitation. Is this a decision that she's going to regret? Du Pré leaves the reader wondering what will be the consequences of this action.

In the following piece from 'A Quiet Evening at Home', a short story by Lisabet Sarai, the central character, Alexandra, discovers her boyfriend has been seeing another woman: Lucia. Along with the other woman, Alexandra hatches a plot to exact a revenge on Michael.

Painfully confused, Michael looked from one of us to the other. His hands clenched in indecision. 'No, I didn't mean that . . . I don't know. I want you both.' His voice took on a pleading quality. 'Please. I don't know what to do.'

'Okay,' I said. 'Then we will tell you. If you obey, then maybe one of us will decide to stay with you. Maybe even both of us. But if you resist, baby, we're gone. Out the door. And out of your life forever. Got it?'

Sarai, L., 'A Quiet Evening at Home'

It sounds here as though Alexandra has already made Michael's decision for him. But in reality this is one of those moments where the reader needs to continue with the story to find out which decision a character has made. Is Michael going to submit to whatever Alexandra and Lucia have planned? Or does Michael have ideas of his own?

EXERCISE

One character has tossed a coin to resolve an internal dilemma: *Head's I'll do it. Tails I won't.* As the coin spins in the air the character briefly contemplates the options.

Decide on the two potential consequences of that coin toss and write down this character's thoughts as she or he tries to decide which would be preferable.

Backstory

As has been said before, it's a common practice to start a story *in medias res* – in the middle of things. A novel will begin with an action scene where characters are involved in a scene, or those characters are engaged in a scene that hooks our interest. It's only in a subsequent chapter where the author reveals the motives and desires that were fuelling that scene through the use of backstory. But there are some points that need to be remembered about backstory.

- Backstory needs to fit seamlessly into the story.

- Backstory should still be presented to the reader through showing – not telling.

- Backstory doesn't have to slow the pace of a story.

There's an art to writing backstory so that it forges an appropriate balance between showing and telling. In the passage below from *Named and Shamed*, Janine Ashbless has achieved that balance by demonstrating that Tansy, the central character in this adult fairy tale, has taken a manuscript from a collector.

I didn't mean to steal the poem, I swear. I just wanted to copy it, and show it to a friend of mine at the university library who knows Victorian Manuscripts. So she could tell me whether it was for real, you understand. There were details in the poem . . . It could be important. I didn't mean to get Edmund Blakey into trouble.

They call it TWOC-ing in legal circles, don't they: Taking Without Owner's Consent. Not theft. Theft means you don't plan to return

it. I had no interest in the monetary value of the manuscript.
And I had every intention of getting it back to Edmund Blakey
before midnight, when the ogre returned.

Ashbless, J., *Named and Shamed*

Notice how Ashbless delivers this backstory from Tansy's point
of view. This is not an invisible narrator telling the reader what's
happened. This is the central character fretting because she
made a wrong decision and she's about to suffer negative
consequences. Notice also how this passage develops Tansy's
character.

♦ We come away from this aware that Tansy is honest: *I didn't*
mean to steal the poem/I had every intention of getting it
back . . .

♦ We come away from this passage having learnt that she is
intelligent: she has friends at the university and she discusses
legal jargon with obvious knowledge.

♦ We come away from this passage having discovered that
Tansy bridges a world between our own substantial world of
universities, manuscripts and legalities and the fairy tale world
of ogres.

This is a lot of detail to include in a short passage and it enriches
the story by developing character as well as building essential
backstory. The following passage shows how backstory is
handled by Gwen Masters:

She wandered through her little apartment and thought about
him, about what it would be like to have him in the hallway,
right here. How broad would his shoulders look between the
walls? How tall would he be? Though she knew Ronaldo, she had
never met him. She had seen pictures of him, but that was
nothing like seeing him in the flesh.

A chance meeting over the Internet brought them together. He
was struggling. So was she. They found a common thread on a
message board, then even more commonality when they began
to talk one-on-one. They discovered oddly parallel lives, the trials
and the same joys, two thousand miles away from each other.

She found herself spending more time on the computer than she should have, because just beyond that screen, Ronaldo was there.

Masters, G., 'Better than Brazil'

In the two paragraphs of this passage, Gwen Masters tells us about the history between the central character and Ronaldo. We get the impression of the trust building through their online romance and the narrator's obvious investment in this fledgling relationship. Masters brushes over insignificant details such as the browser the character used, or the website where they made that first accidental encounter. These details are extraneous and would dilute the impact of the story being told. Instead, Masters writes as though the reader understands technology as complex as message boards and is already aware of the unspoken dangers of internet relationships.

EXERCISE

Take one of your previous exercises that involved the opening to a story. Focus on one character and explain something important about that character's background. Either explain why they made a particular decision that had bearing on the piece you wrote, or explain what led them to be in the place they were when the story started. Don't be afraid to write extensively and then edit and revise to lose unimportant detail.

Passage of time

Readers want to explore a full and vivid storyworld and share all the excitement being experienced by the characters they've met in your story. They don't want to be bored by tedious and irrelevant scenes or uninspiring minutiae. Sometimes, even when a character is doing exciting things, it can be useful to show the swift passage of time to prevent readers from growing weary of irrelevant or repetitive scenes.

❛ Alfred Hitchcock observed that good drama was "life with the dull bits cut out". As maxims go, it's a useful one to observe when writing the middle section of any piece of fiction. ❜

The following, from Justine Elyot's *Game*, shows how it's possible to touch on the passage of time without detailing every narrative moment. Elyot's story is character driven but this brief focus on the cause and effect of the developing plot demonstrates how a writer can maintain an overview of what's occurring in the story without allowing the details to overpower the reader or without letting the narrative become dull or repetitive.

Day four involves a butt plug. On day five I'm tied to the bed and tickled with feather dusters until I scream.

But what really worries me is day six.

On day six he does nothing at all.

I wake up in his bed on day seven insouciant and breezy.

'Almost there,' I crow, ignoring my morning fog of lust and jumping out of bed.

'Almost,' says Lloyd, watching me from the bed. 'Not quite.'

'What have you got planned? I can't believe you didn't try anything on yesterday. You must have some kind of massive finale prepared.'

'You know me too well.' He's quiet for a moment, watching me scoop my shower things out of my overnight bag. He's told me thousands of times I should keep some on his shelf, but I've never got round to it. 'I've invited some friends round for dinner.'

I stand straight, watching his face for a moment. 'Oh?'

'Close friends.'

'Who?'

'Rachael and O from the club.'

'For dinner?'

'Yeah. It's our day off. Thought they could come round in the afternoon and hang out.'

'And by hang out, you mean . . . ?'

'You'll see.'

Elyot, J., *Game*

This passage allows the reader to see that four days of Sophie's week-long sexual obligation to Martin have passed, without allowing the reader to grow tired by the repetitiveness of the ordeal. This passage maintains the focus on sexual variety and endurance, introduces the promise of a *ménage* episode, and all without letting the reader become bored.

EXERCISE

You're writing a story about a couple spending seven days together. On the first day they seem to break every taboo. You have saved something special for them to enjoy on the seventh night. But the rest of what they are likely to do together will be a repeat of encounters already enjoyed on that first day.

Use no more than a couple of paragraphs to show that this couple remain sexually active and interested in one another, but without allowing the reader to become bored by repetition.

In the end

❝ Theorists used to discuss the Greek unities or Aristotle's unities. It's since been realised that these 'unities' are a neoclassical conceit only loosely based on a misinterpretation of Aristotle's *Poetics*. Nevertheless, it's worth considering them as they apply to endings because they can be a useful tool for anyone working to the discipline of a plot. ❞

Unity of time

A story should take place over no more than 24 hours.

This condition made sense during the days when fiction was performed on stage. Although it now seems to have fallen out of fashion, there is something comforting about stories that are compartmentalised into the events of a year, a season, a month, a day or a single afternoon.

Unity of place

A story should start and finish in the same geographical location.

This one was important during Aristotle's days, particularly when plays were being performed on stages that didn't have scenery or any way of conveying a change of location. However, novels do not require this particular unity.

Nevertheless, in Lisette Ashton's erotic novel *Beyond Temptation*, the story begins with a scene where a cuckolded husband is walking up the stairs of his home, about to walk in on his wife with her lover. The story ends in a different house several hundred miles away from this starting point, but with that same husband walking up a set of stairs on the brink of catching his wife involved in another illicit encounter. To a great extent it could be argued that this story's beginning and ending fulfil the requirements of unity of place.

Unity of action

A story should have one main action with no or few subplots.

It makes sense to have a story focus on one particular character but it's difficult to imagine any contemporary story of length without subplots. Subplots can help to show contrasting reactions to a particular situation. Subplots can help to relieve any build up of tension or can be used to show facets of a story that would be otherwise unknown to the reader. When concluding a story, it's always wisest to have the conclusion of the main story – the main action – as the final detail.

Regardless of whether a writer is trying to apply these unities, the end of a story should always be complete and satisfying. It should always leave the reader sure that:

◆ they know what will immediately happen to the characters;

◆ there is no more story to be told;

◆ the majority of important questions raised at the beginning have now been addressed.

It's always possible to leave an opportunity for a sequel, or a series of follow-up titles. But this should never be done at the expense of a conclusive ending.

EXERCISE

Take any of your starting points from earlier in this chapter and write the logical conclusion. Is your writing obeying any of the unities mentioned here? Has the story taken place over a specific period of time? Are events developing so that they start and end in the same place? Does this conclusion fulfil a unity of action?

Summary

◆ Outline your plot in note form to begin with.

◆ Follow existing templates of stories but always make sure you give the narrative your own distinctive spin.

◆ On writing beginnings:
  ◇ Experiment with detailed, expository beginnings.
  ◇ Experiment with attention-grabbing beginnings.
  ◇ Experiment by starting a story *in medias res.*
  ◇ Experiment with other styles of openings until you find one that suits your style and complements the story you want to tell.

◆ On writing middles:
  ◇ Remember that plots are built through a process of action and reaction.
  ◇ Use the middle of a narrative to feed backstory to your reader.
  ◇ Use the middle of a narrative to show the swift passage of time when this is necessary to avoid showing repetition.
  ◇ Remember Hitchcock's words: *Drama is life with the dull bits cut out.*

◆ On writing endings:
  ◇ Aspire to follow the Greek unities if they apply to your writing.
  ◇ Feel free to ignore the Greek unities if they don't apply.
  ◇ It doesn't matter whether you're writing a happy ending or a tragic conclusion – as long as that final scene satisfies your reader so they know there is no more story to be told this time.

NOTE: Be aware that plotting and outlining can stifle creativity in some writers. If plotting doesn't work for you as a writer, tell the story in a way that does work for you without resorting to these tactics. If plotting does work for you, don't neglect this vital step in the process of getting your work written.

Developing your powers of description

6

THE ROLE OF DESCRIPTION IN FICTION

On one level description can simply be the written portrayal of how the story's events are perceived through the six senses (sight, sound, taste, smell, touch and feelings). On other levels, description can be used to suggest mood or indicate how a character feels about a particular situation or it can be used to change the pace of a story.

> ❛ Description in fiction is used to give the reader a greater sense of the storyworld's reality or physicality. This is particularly appropriate in erotica where readers often approach this genre for descriptions of characters involved in the most physical interactions. ❜

A word of warning

◆ Description can form the most eloquent and favoured parts of a piece of fiction, or it can consist of the dullest sections that the reader flicks past to get to the 'real' action.

◆ Description can provide aspects that the reader finds most insightful, and it can also be the parts that the reader finds hilariously distracting.

Finding the correct balance between these extremes of boredom and brilliance is the goal of every writer. Achieving that balance every time is a challenge that few of us ever manage.

USING DESCRIPTION EFFECTIVELY

Scott ran his fingers through my hair and told me I was beautiful. When he said it he looked me straight in the eyes. He wouldn't look away until I gave him a response. I knew this, so I stared right back. I took in every detail of his eyes so I would never forget the power behind them. The colour, a blue so magical, as if the ocean and the sky had blended together after a storm. The shape, deep and wide, like the comforting shelter of a mother's womb. I took in his long, feminine lashes and his perfectly arched brows. I could see his honesty, his passion and a mysterious history that held years of unrevealed struggle. When my observations caused an intense fluttering sensation in my stomach, I finally turned up the corners of my mouth, ever so slightly and said, 'Thank you.'

I often wished that Scott and I were the type of people who could fall in love.

Morizawa, J., *Memoirs of a Wannabe Sex Addict*

Morizawa's opening passage here gives us a sharply detailed image of Scott's blue eyes. We don't just get to see their eloquently described colour. We get to see their shape and the lashes and eyebrows framing these eyes. Notice how Morizawa describes Scott's eyes.

◆ We don't know what Scott's lips look like.

◆ We have no idea if Scott is skinny, fat or covered in tattoos.

◆ However, we get such a vivid description of those eyes that no other detail matters because the narrator's description of his eyes tells us Scott is perceived as attractive.

He has feminine lashes and arched eyebrows – features that suggest he is pretty rather than handsome. The shape of his eyes is associated with the maternal shape of a womb, suggesting that the narrator trusts him and feels comfortable in his presence. And all Morizawa has shown us are his eyes.

❢ Notice also the mood that Morizawa sets with this description. Scott's eyes are the colour of the sky and the ocean blending after a storm. The suggestion of these natural phenomena – sky, oceans and storms – is now linked in the reader's mind with Scott's attractive features and his caring personality. ❣

The final line in this passage says:

'I often wished that Scott and I were the type of people who could fall in love . . .'

This is another example of how good writers effectively use description. Morizawa has presented us with the narrator's loving description of Scott. She finishes this with an ironic reference to wishing that they loved each other, when it seems apparent that the narrator, at least, is in love. This intriguing statement begins the story before the reader has become tired of reading too much description.

Some similar techniques are used in the following piece from Saskia Walker:

I turned and took in the sight that met my eyes. Standing in a suspended cradle was a window cleaner moving a large squeegee over the surface of the glass with a rhythmic agility, all the while watching me and grinning cheekily. I managed to return his smile and wave at him, snatching up my cup from the desk to cover my awkwardness.

Something interesting had finally happened! And, yes, he was interesting. Ruggedly good-looking with several days' worth of stubble – tall, well-built, and bleached blond. He went about his work in a showy, nonchalant way that made it look like a warm-up for dirty dancing. He moved his entire body as if dancing to the music he was listening to on his headset, and rode his massive squeegee easily over the surface of the glass, his biceps flexing, his torso riding firm and strong beneath the T-shirt he was wearing. Sexy! My blood pumped quicker when I noticed he was eyeing me speculatively, from head to toe. I leaned one hip up against the desk, toying the mug in my hands, eyeing up the sight. Well, why not? He was doing the same.

When he finished his task, he dropped the squeegee and reached into his pocket and pulled something out. He scribbled on the piece of paper with a stub of pencil, then held it up against the glass for me to read. I stepped closer and read the scrawled message:

GREAT LEGS. NEXT TIME WEAR A SHORT SKIRT.

Walker, S., 'Counting the Days'

Walker gives us a full picture of events here.

♦ We get to see the central character's viewpoint of the window cleaner and all the rich description that makes him appear like the irresistible male hero of an erotic story.

♦ We get to see his muscular build, his ruggedly handsome good looks and we're given a strong sense of the narrator's interest in this character.

♦ She describes him as being attractive and, consequently, we can see that she is attracted to him.

But notice how this description is as much as we get before Walker moves the story along. She describes him in breathtaking detail. And then we're moved on to read the window cleaner's note and consider its consequences in the story being told.

♦ The attractive couple in Walker's story have now met.

♦ The next step is for them to take their relationship up a level.

♦ Walker doesn't bore her readers with unnecessary description. She is moving on from this point to make sure her readers continue enjoying everything she has to tell them.

EXERCISE

Describe someone you like and know well. This can be a character from your fiction or a friend or family member. Select one aspect of their appearance and describe that detail as vividly as you can in positive terms. Tell your reader about the shape and the colour of that one aspect of the person. Tell your reader about the size and any other dimensions you think are appropriate. Concentrate solely on the appearance of that one feature and constantly remind yourself that you're describing this feature in positive terms because it's an aspect of someone you like.

Repeat this exercise to show a fictional character admiring someone she or he likes. Have that character describe a single feature of a person they find attractive. Write this piece without boldly stating that she or he is attracted to this character. Suggest the character's attraction by describing features in positive terms.

ENRICHING YOUR WRITING BY INVOLVING ALL THE SENSES

As was mentioned before, we describe using six senses:

◆ Sight

◆ Sound

◆ Smell

◆ Taste

◆ Touch

◆ Emotions/feelings

Of the six senses sight is the one most commonly described in fiction, followed by sound. However, by not reminding the reader about smell, taste and touch, writers are missing out on the opportunity to make the storyworlds they create into fuller experiences.

❛ In writing about emotions or feelings, telling the reader whether a character is happy or sad, excited or bored, etc., there is a strong danger that a story is being *told* rather than *shown*. However, because we need to convey this information to the reader, it's always worth trying to include some description about these senses, even if the suggestion of emotion is only implied. ❜

That night was hot. The blanket was scratchy against my naked body. We'd washed our clothes in our bathwater, and they were still drying. Several of the women snored. And my body hadn't gotten enough. I could hear Delilah's even, deep breathing within easy arm's reach and could picture her beautiful breasts rising up and down with each breath. I remembered the way her triangle had felt against my toes and the quick grind of her callused heel against my sex before it moved away. I nearly reached for her but touched myself instead. It was wet fire down there. I made it burn brighter and brighter, until I bit my lip to keep from moaning. I shuddered over and over, until finally my fingers traced a sticky, lazy path back up my stomach, my hands relaxed, and a deep sleep held me close and rocked me.

Levy, C., 'Independence'

Levy gives us a strong sense of the physicality of this story set in the times of the American Civil War.

- We're told that the night is hot.

- We're told that the blanket is scratchy against the narrator's naked body.

- She says '*It was wet fire down there.*'

- Once she has satisfied her arousal, her fingers trace '*a sticky, lazy path back up*' her stomach.

Throughout this passage Levy keeps us involved with the physicality that her central character is enjoying so that we can share that sensory experience and she doesn't just rely on sight and sounds.

Donna George Storey immerses her reader in this same level of rich detail in her novel *Amorous Woman*:

I tipped forward, an invisible hand pressing me toward her. I found her lips and closed my eyes. We stayed like that for a moment, barely touching. I could go no farther myself. Chieko was the one to open and welcome me into her. Her lips were very soft indeed. Our tongues met. I tasted somen noodles, the sweetness of the dipping sauce, a hint of her saliva. Chieko brought her hand to my cheek and we melted closer, but then she seemed content to linger, just as we were.

This isn't a man, what the hell do I do? What are the rules?

The words swirled through my head, but strangely, I sensed I didn't have to do anything but be. *It was, in fact, not like kissing a man at all. There was no face stubble, no tongue snaking deep as a preview of coming attractions, no conquest, no yielding. All boundaries gave way to the softness. Even the desk under my ass seemed to dissolve into a cushion of air leaving my body suspended, just like Chieko's story with no ending.*

Storey, D. G., *Amorous Woman*

Here, Storey shows us a kiss between two women that has become powerfully erotic. Again we have the experience presented to us with very little concern for the sight and sound of what's going on.

◆ Storey's narrator talks about the delicate flavour of Chieko's last meal, still resting on her lips.

◆ She talks about the softness of Chieko's lips.

◆ She even discusses the differences between this kiss from a woman and kisses she has previously experienced with men.

Aside from addressing the narrator's surprise to discover herself kissing someone of the same sex, this description immerses the reader in the character's physical response to the experience. It is the mixture of touch, taste, sight and smell and the character's reaction to those experiences that brings this work to life.

'Wait,' she says. Without moving away from the wall, she opens her purse and pulls out a purple package. She rips it open and spreads a thin sheet of latex between her legs. 'I'll hold it,' she says, and she does, with one hand in front and one in back. I'm a little disappointed – I'd wanted to taste her – but I'm grateful too. And when I put my tongue against her, I can still feel her heat even through the dam. The latex tastes like vanilla, but beneath that, I can smell her own caramel and chocolate sweetness. She is already wet and loose, open enough that I can slide my tongue across the sweet warm caramel of her, run it from back to front. Her clit is easy to find – already pointed and nubby. I run over the point of it with the flat of my tongue and she slides down lower, presses herself against me.

Germain, S., 'All About the Girls'

We can see here in this passage how Germain vividly portrays the use of a dental dam for cunnilingus. We get a strong sense of pleasurable erotic scents and the narrator's muted sense of frustration at this move towards safe sex. But there is never a moment in this piece where we don't get a full sense of the physical intimacy that's occurring between these two characters.

EXERCISE

Describe a scene that's about to develop into oral sex. Show two characters kissing, touching and exploring. Then move onto those first steps where the intimacy grows more explicit. Use a vocabulary with which you and your characters are comfortable. Feel free to describe sights and sounds in this scene but, for the purposes of this exercise, try to focus here on the character's experiences of smell, taste and touch. Make this a sex-positive scene and write with vivid attention to the physical detail being enjoyed.

CREATING ARRESTING IMPRESSIONS: EROTICISING CLOTHES, FURNINSHINGS AND OTHER DETAILS

It's not just bodies and acts of sexuality that are described in erotic fiction. Clothes, furnishings and other features of the real world can be eroticised. The following examples show how the description of clothing can be used to eroticise scenarios.

Mei adjusted the red and gold lacquer chopsticks holding her black hair in a tight chignon. She applied just a bit more rouge to her lips, but nothing else. Her porcelain skin and dark eyes needed no embellishment other than the pinch of a cheek to add the hint of rose.

Her black and red dress had dragons woven into the silk in golden thread. She had adapted the design of the dress from some of the newer styles she'd seen in China, but she had gone much further than was even the least bit proper. The style really was quite shocking. It had a high collar, split in the middle, and long fitted sleeves. The dress hugged her breasts and cinched in

naturally at her waist. The hemline came only to midcalf,
showing the loose, black silk trousers she wore underneath. Both
sides of the formfitting skirt were slit from hem to knee, making
it easier to move. Her current experiment called for the charming
and seduction of young men, and the style of her dress helped
immensely.

King, D. L., 'The Treatment'

In this description King is giving us an overview of Mei's oriental
outfit but she constantly keeps the clothing eroticised.

- The reds in the clothing complement the colour of Mei's
  cheeks if she pinches them.

- The dress hugs Mei's breasts and cinches her waist.

- The clothing here is not just hanging on Mei's body but it's
  intimately interacting with the woman wearing those clothes.

In many ways this will be seen as a precursor to the way another
character will interact with Mei as the story develops.

So I showed up with two bags of dirty laundry, hair piled on top
of my head and feeling rather frightful. I had thrown on a pair
of sling-back heels and sweater that matched my skirt. I looked
at my reflection in the glass door and thought this wasn't exactly
the kind of thing most people would wear to the laundromat. I
just didn't have time to think about what I was wearing and
most of my favourite things were in these bags. And anyway,
there was just one other person in the laundromat besides me.

DooLittle, D., 'Clean Panties'

DooLittle takes us into a story here where a character has turned
up at the laundromat dressed in those few clothes remaining
from her wardrobe that are clean and presentable. We get an
overview of someone with haphazard hair, inappropriate heels
and a sweater that loosely matches her skirt. And while this tells
us nothing about colour, size, shape or any of the other details
we associate with description, it gives us the impression of
someone who doesn't particularly care about fashion or style. It
gives us an overview of the story's central character.

❛ For those who are wondering how this could possibly be construed as being erotic:

◆ DooLittle's character is now alone in the laundromat with just one other person.

◆ A laundromat is a venue where private garments are on semi-public display.

◆ This suggestion of unwitting exhibitionism lends itself to a story of developing sexual excitement. ❜

She'd been in bed, wearing her favourite negligee – her only negligee, truth be told, but still her favourite – with its deep, dark blue silk, the kind that could make anyone want to get lost in it, the kind that spoke of the ocean and ink and lust. It accentuated her pale skin, complemented the light freckles that tickled her cheeks, and with her lips stained dark, bloodlike red, she knew the contrast was striking.

Though Frankie couldn't appreciate the sight of her negligee during phone sex, he could certainly appreciate her description of it. And honestly, Kate put it on more to get herself in the mood. It had worked, all too well. She was extremely horny and she smiled to herself, lying prone in bed. She could practically taste Frankie's cock as she listened to the phone ring.

Bussel, R. K., 'Blow Me'

In this extract Bussel is showing us a character about to engage in phone sex.

◆ We get an overview of the woman's negligee.

◆ We get a description of how the blue complements the central character's skin tones.

◆ We're told it's the colour of the ocean and ink and lust. Each one of those layers of blue seems to become darker and darker.

◆ The almost black-like blue of the negligee is then contrasted against the narrator's pale complexion and her blood-red lipstick.

This is a rich palate of colours that creates a vivid and striking image on which the reader can focus.

> ### EXERCISE
>
> 1. Your narrator is sitting in a bar and admires a smartly dressed stranger. Describe this scene from the narrator's point of view. Make the clothes appear sexy through describing their colour and the way they fit the stranger's build. Write this scene until the point where the narrator decides she or he needs to approach the stranger.
> 2. Your narrator has just woken up at the start of a long weekend. There is no pressure to dress for work or to wear anything other than comfortable clothes. How does your narrator dress? Describe her or him getting ready for the day. And then show her or his reaction on discovering a forgotten lover asleep on the couch.

USING FIGURATIVE LANGUAGE TO BRING CHARACTERS AND SCENES TO LIFE

> 'Fondling,' she saith, 'since I have hemm'd thee here
> Within the circuit of this ivory pale,
> I'll be a park, and thou shalt be my deer;
> Feed where thou wilt, on mountain or in dale:
> Graze on my lips; and if those hills be dry,
> Stray lower, where the pleasant fountains lie.
>
> Shakespeare, W., 'Venus and Adonis'

In this verse from Shakespeare's poem 'Venus and Adonis', we can see the poet making use of an extended metaphor.

- Venus describes Adonis as a deer.

- Venus extends this poetic conceit by offering her own body as a park.

- The metaphor is further extended by Venus's suggestion that Adonis (the deer) should feed *on mountain or in dale*.

- Venus adds, *if those hills be dry, stray lower where the pleasant fountains lie*.

This is delightfully suggestive poetry from the most celebrated writer in the English language. It's also a perfect example of how figurative language can be used within erotica.

❛ Description is where writers are able to make comparisons using the figurative language of similes and metaphors. This figurative language can bring a piece to life. The writer is allowed to tell the story using their own choice of words and images. This can set a mood and tone that is appropriate for the characters in the fiction and the story being told. In the verse from Shakespeare above, the associations of deer foraging in a park present pleasant images of the natural order of events. ❜

He wasn't pretty. It wasn't that he was ugly. No, he had great lines that reminded her of something out of a book on Greek mythology she'd had as a kid: straight nose, square jaw, wide forehead. He looked hard. His arms were so inked it looked like he was wearing flesh-coloured gloves. His skin had been a tapestry he had kept covering with an assortment of images that ranged from the grotesque to the racy to the beautiful. Rex was about as straight and narrow as they came, but he looked like a badass and that just did things to Denise.

Hartnett, A.M., 'Safe for Work'

Rex is portrayed here as having great lines that '*reminded her of something out of a book on Greek mythology*'. This is Hartnett's stylish way of saying that Rex looked like a Greek god but without resorting to such a cliché. She uses a simile to describe his untattooed hands in contrast to the rest of his body:

'*His arms were so inked it looked like he was wearing flesh-coloured gloves.*'

It's an effective simile because it's original and it allows us to see the paleness of his hands set against his tattooed arms in an unusual way. When Harnett says '*his skin had been a tapestry*' we understand that this narrator is not someone who thinks tattoos are inelegant graffiti. This is the opinion of an aficionado who has elevated the appreciation of ink on skin (particularly the ink on Rex's skin) to art criticism.

She eased Tara down into the cushions and kissed and caressed her breasts until her nipples felt like stalagmites rising up from the cave, a thought that, under the circumstances, didn't really seem all that strange. Sky knew that the herbs Tara had taken in the mulled wine earlier were already thinning the veil between the physical world and the Dream World, while heightening her senses at the same time. She had never known her coven leader to call upon so much powerful magic for something that should have been a simple dream encounter, and that made her more than a little nervous. Sky could hear Tara's breath like a wind in the cave as she kissed down her belly and opened her legs, which she no longer had the will to do for herself.

Grace, K. D., *Body Temperature and Rising*

In this passage we can see that Grace is using figurative language to describe Tara's arousal. But we can also see that Grace is using the figurative language to make Tara's arousal reflect the natural (and supernatural) beauty of the Lakeland area where this story takes place.

◆ Tara's nipples point up '*like stalagmites*'.

◆ Her breath sounds '*like a wind in the cave*'.

It's an effective way to remind the reader that Tara is involved with a coven of elemental forces, all at one with nature, and her sexuality is inseparable from that natural relationship.

EXERCISE

As mentioned before, figurative language is the area where a writer can describe a story in terms that are appropriate for particular characters in specific circumstances. Keeping this relationship between appropriate analogies reinforces the information and the suspicions a reader already has about a character, making the storyworld more vivid and the fiction, ultimately, stronger.

Write three sex scenes and use figurative language within those scenes to convey a sense of character and a sense of place. Try writing the following:

- an outdoor scene set in all-natural surroundings;

- an indoor scene in a cosmopolitan city apartment bedroom;

- a fantasy scene in the highest turret of a castle.

Use at least one character from the following list:

- power-hungry executive;

- an heir to a position of privilege;

- someone with a dark secret;

- a person hiding their true identity;

- someone about to have sex for money;

- an erstwhile faithful character about to have an affair.

Allow the character's situation and the location to influence your description.

SUMMARY

- Description involves using all six senses:
  - Sight;
  - Sound;
  - Smell;
  - Taste;
  - Touch;
  - Emotions/feelings.

- Effective description finds a balance between too much and too little description.

- Describing one single detail of a character will be more effective than describing every aspect of their appearance.

- Aside from describing characters in an erotic fashion, clothes, locations and most other details can be described with some level of arousing content.

- The figurative language of similes and metaphors can reinforce aspects of a story to make it more compelling.

Writing great dialogue 7

MAKING SEX TALK CONVINCING

'I tried to avoid him, Daniel, I swear. I really, really did. But he came begging for it. He followed me, for God's sake! I'm not that strong. No one is. If you could have seen him, you'd be a little more understanding! He was irresistible, Daniel . . .'

'Tell me you cleaned up properly, Marta. Just tell me that,' he said, with a low, measured voice, levelling his gaze at me.

'Well, in a sense, yes.'

Daniel's hand flew out and grabbed my throat. 'What the fuck does that mean?' He yanked me toward him, his face only inches from mine.

'Well, actually . . . he's outside in the hall,' I wheezed.

'You irresponsible bitch'! The final consonant sprayed my face with his saliva. 'You turned him?'

Remittance Girl, 'Midnight at Sheremetyevo'

Good dialogue bridges the gap between the flat world of written text and the reality of the spoken word as it should be heard by a listener. Good dialogue is at the core of every well-received story and is essential in erotic fiction.

❝ One of the most repeated criticisms pitched against dialogue in erotic media is that it's unconvincing. This point was often made by critics condemning *Fifty Shades of Grey* but that book is not the first piece of erotica to suffer such accusations. ❞

- Connoisseurs of adult films repeatedly complain of pointless conversations.

- Editors of erotica frequently bemoan the single syllable exchanges that make sex scenes so banal such as, 'Ugh'! and 'Yeah'! and 'Wow'!

- Readers complain regularly about asinine interjections spoiling otherwise engaging material.

The effective portrayal of spoken words on the page can prove to be a huge hurdle for any writer trying to convincingly relay a conversation to the reader. The skill of writing dialogue, particularly the skill of writing *good dialogue*, is one of the main challenges that should be mastered by anyone wishing to write credible erotic fiction. No one expects the fictional participants of a sexually explicit encounter to exchange pithy views on Keats or Kierkegaard. Yet most readers would prefer characters who can say something worthy of maintaining a reader's interest.

Dialogue is a lot more than the words a character says. Dialogue can include:

- what is said;

- how it's said;

- who is speaking;

- why it's being said;

- what's not being said.

EXERCISE

Write down two lists of exclamations a character would be likely to use at the height of passion in a sex scene. For the first list write down a list of things a female character would be likely to say. For the second list write down a list of things a male character would be likely to say.

Keep these lists safe.

Now write down two lists of topics characters are likely to discuss during a passionate sex scene.

◆ Be pragmatic if you want: *Does that ceiling need another coat of paint?*

◆ Be philosophical if you want: *Is this what's meant by the pleasure principle?*

◆ Be realistic: *Have we got time to do this if you need to be up early in the morning?*

Do any of these exchanges strike you as being appropriate for an erotic scene? Which ones would work for the type of story you want to tell?

PRESENTING DIALOGUE ON THE PAGE

'Ah, by God's barren balls!' exclaimed Curval. 'That's a splendid passion indeed; yet I must say, it could be improved upon.'

'Oh? How?' asked Durcet, his voice betraying his arousal.

'How?' repeated Curval. 'Why, by the choice of food and partner.'

'The partner? Ah yes, of course; you'd prefer the likes of Fanchon.'

'Absolutely!'

'And the food?' Durcet continued, as Adelaide massaged his cock and balls.

Marquis de Sade, *120 Days of Sodom*

The mechanics of dialogue are fairly straightforward. The basic rules are:

◆ Every word of dialogue should be included between speech marks.

◆ Each new speaker is given a new paragraph.

◆ All punctuation relating to the spoken words, including question marks, exclamation marks and commas, is contained within those speech marks.

EXERCISE

Read dialogue from a favourite passage of erotica and note how the author has presented this conversation on the page. Note how the 'spoken' words are contained within speech marks. Note how attributions (*he said, she said, asked Durcet, repeated Curval*) are used to make sure the reader knows who is talking. Note how attributions are sometimes avoided to speed up the pace of an exchange. As you're reading these passages, focus on the mechanics of how the dialogue is being presented rather than the message that is being conveyed by the characters.

NOW WE'RE REALLY TALKING

Accents and dialects

'We're Bohunks. What're you?'

Lon turned from the wheel, guessing at the question's meaning. 'Welsh and English descent.'

'Well, we're Bohem'an. My real first name is Fialka. That means Vi'let. My last name's Polivka. You know what that means? Soup. Vi'let Soup. Ain't that a kill? Vi'let Soup.'

Some of the tension eased away. Lon could laugh at this.

'Guys usta say, "How's about a little hot soup?" Horka polivka. Jeez, it usta make me so mad.' She remembered another important factor. 'We're Cath'lic. You Cath'lic?'

Martin, D., Twilight Girl

This exchange between Violet and Lon comes early on in the story and we quickly get to understand the rhythms of Violet's distinctive accent.

❛ Accents are usually introduced with the character's first piece of dialogue. The reader would undoubtedly be perplexed to discover that a character introduced in Chapter 1 has been speaking with a broad Irish brogue that isn't mentioned until halfway through Chapter 48. ❜

There are several different ways accents can be treated on the page.

◆ The suggestion of an accent can be made through phonemic deviation:

'Ah cannae hold 'er, cap'n!'

◆ The presence of an accent could be indicated with a reference in the narrative:

'I can't hold her, Captain,' he cried – excitement sharpening his Scottish accent.

The general rule in writing fiction is to aim for clarity and keep the text accessible for the reader. *'Ah cannae hold 'er, cap'n!'* might accurately represent a character's specific intonation and pronunciation. But this attention to detail has to be weighed against the importance of the reader understanding what's been said. With this example the reader is concentrating less on what is being said and more on the way it is being spoken.

If this factor is of importance to the story (for example, the story shows the speaker is an ardent *Star Trek* fan, and the speaker being a fan of that TV series is relevant to the story) then it's the right way to do it. However, if this is merely an affectation for the writer's amusement then it will be a distraction for the reader and should have no place within well-constructed dialogue.

EXERCISE

Take any snatches of dialogue from your writing and rewrite so the words appear to have been spoken with an obvious accent or dialect. Take time to make sure each word can only be pronounced in one particular way. Leave this passage to settle for a day or a week and then return to it.

- ◆ Does it still seem as clear?

- ◆ Or is there a strong element of confusion now as you try to work out what was being said?

- ◆ If you were reading this passage, would you find it accessible or confusing?

Stress, pitch and italics

Vocal stress and specific emphasis is another trait of the spoken word that does not transfer easily to the written page. The three words, 'I want you,' can be given specific emphasis by italicising any of the individual words to imply different meanings:

- ◆ '*I* want you.'

- ◆ 'I *want* you.'

- ◆ 'I want *you*.'

The first of these examples would be useful for a character to clarify their desires in conversation with a potential partner who is unaware of their interest.

- ◆ 'No one here is remotely interested in me,' John complained. Jane shook her head. '*I* want you.'

The second is more emphatic, expressing a stressed desire where the need for the other person is more important than the people involved.

- ◆ 'Is something troubling you?' John asked. Jane lowered her voice to a whisper. 'I *want* you.'

The third variation, like the first, allows a character to explicitly clarify their desires for a particular partner.

- ◆ 'Which of us had you been trying to attract?' John asked. Jane blushed but met his gaze with defiance. 'I want *you*.'

It should be noted here that emphasis through italics has more impact when the technique is used sparingly. If italics are used too often, they cease to have the same effect.

EXERCISE

Go back to the list of exclamations you made earlier in this chapter. Try to write a couple of the exclamations from each list so that they can only be read as passionate exclamations. Make sure you make notes for the pauses. Make sure you annotate where the stresses should be.

Alternatively, look at the three ways listed above of expressing different sentiments with the words 'I want you'. Try to write one of these exchanges into a full scene.

Contractions

On the stage, the young man's head was pushed down and his hips tugged up. He was being arranged by his aggressor, handled like he was nothing more than a bendable sex toy. He glanced up at the audience. His eyes were wild, full of fear. The bald man put his foot to the younger man's shaggy head and pushed it back down.

'He's afraid, Donna!'

'Shh. Don't be silly. They're lovers.'

'In real life?'

'Yes. This is what they do. Don't you study drama?'

'Yeah.' Sarah wanted to look away, but she couldn't, she was riveted by the passion play taking place on the stage.

'So. It's a play. A sex play. OK?'

Moore, M., *Sarah's Education*

In this extract from *Sarah's Education* we see how Moore efficiently conveys the sense of genuine conversation in her dialogue. When Moore is not writing erotica she works on screenplays, so her knowledge of the conventions for writing convincing dialogue is second to none.

◆ Note how the majority of sentences include contractions, such as 'Don't' and 'They're'. This reflects most people's natural laziness when speaking.

◆ Note how Moore doesn't need to rely on speech tags such as *she said* or *he said*, or *they asked*, etc. It's established in Sarah's first line of dialogue that she's talking to Donna. After that, because there are only two of them in the conversation, the reader never has any doubt as to which character is speaking.

◆ Note also that this exchange is made in a whispered tone, all of which is suggested by the fact that they are watching a 'sex play' and Donna's first instruction to Sarah was for her to shush.

Contractions within dialogue make a character's voice appear more credible and convincing. Consider the difference between the following:

'You do not know what you are saying.'
'You don't know what you're saying.'

The first of these is more formal and rigid. It doesn't sound like natural speech and, unless a character is speaking in this robotic fashion to emphasise a particular emotion (or an absence of emotion), the reader will pick up on the dialogue's artificiality and be removed from the fiction.

The second of these examples reads more like natural speech with the contracted 'don't' and 'you're' reflecting the genuine rhythms and patterns of elision.

EXERCISE

Write a passionate dialogue exchange where characters speak with unrealistic formality. Make this a scene where two characters are declaring their ardent desire for each other. However, in this scene, do not write 'didn't' or 'would've' or 'shan't'. Instead write 'did not' or 'would have' or 'shall not'.

Consider this exchange objectively. Does it appear stilted, unnatural and robotic? Now rewrite this scene applying contractions and removing unnecessary words wherever possible. Which piece of dialogue best suits the style you want for your fiction?

Speech tags and modifiers

'Why the fuck didn't you call me, Shawn?'

'Because you asked me not to.'

'I know what I asked you, but—'

'But what? Was I not supposed to believe you?'

'Well, yes, but if you cared at all, I thought you might have at least called to check and see if I was okay.'

'Why wouldn't you be? You told me it was what you wanted.'

'It was.' She hung her head. She was embarrassed now.

Shawn shrugged. 'Well?'

Lynn threw her hands up and the words came spilling from her lips.

Brown, T., 'Cling'

❝ The current vogue in writing, as illustrated in the above passage, stands against the overuse of speech tags and modifiers in dialogue. While it is occasionally helpful to say, John complained; Jane asked; he stammered; or she exclaimed (etc.), it is acknowledged that these verbs should be redundant if the dialogue has been well crafted and is fulfilling its function correctly. ❞

In this passage we're aware that two people are talking: Shawn and Lynn. Lynn mentions Shawn's name in the opening line of this exchange. After that the author doesn't worry about saying *Shawn said this* or *Lynn said that*.

Tenille Brown treats her readers with respect.

◆ It's obvious that Shawn is not giving voice to that opening line because his name is mentioned just before the question mark.

◆ It's equally obvious that Shawn would be responding to the question asked of him in the opening line – so readers should know he is replying.

Brown makes this fast-paced exchange easy to follow, with little need for attribution or speech tags. We read one line of dialogue. We know that the next line is from the other person involved in the exchange.

EXERCISE

Create a scene where two characters converse. Keep the dialogue believable using contractions and elision where possible. Try and keep the speech tags to a minimum.

◆ How long can you keep the exchange going without needing to add speech tags?

◆ Does the dialogue remain clear?

◆ Is it still obvious who's talking or is there some confusion?

◆ If there is any confusion, what can you do to rectify this?

ENTICING YOUR READER

'What about someone like George? You were wetting your knickers for him.'

'Cheek! I was not'!

'Oh no? I saw the way you were looking at him. Don't blame you, though. Sexy voice.'

'Who, me?' Max walked in with a tray loaded with glasses, jugs and bottles held just above his still hard cock, like a male version of a Playboy bunny.

'No, your mate George. I was telling Nina they could be made for each other.'

'Piss off, Ange,' Nina helped herself to a glass full of orange juice and drank deeply. 'That's better. I would like to remind you both that being brought off by Max just now notwithstanding, I have a very good relationship going already. This night's a one-off.'

'Shame,' said Max, grinning. 'Hope that means you're going to make it one to remember.'

'Thought I already had,' said Nina with raised eyebrows. 'I suppose you're thinking of your own selfish orgasm.'

Hamilton, L., *Fire & Ice*

Where dialogue is concerned, it's always worth remembering your reader. Readers scan books looking for dialogue. Readers are particularly keen to search for dialogue:

- if a story has grown stale;

- if there's too much description;

- if the plot has become wearisome.

For some reason, possibly because there's a lot of white space on the page, dialogue catches the eye and allows readers to stop. It could be that readers know dialogue conveys a lot of plot, character and story in very little space, so they're prepared to stop for that reason. It's worth remembering, whenever there's a chance to include dialogue, your readers will appreciate the opportunity to stop and enjoy hearing your characters speak.

> ❝ As with all matters in creating enjoyable fiction, the onus is on the writer to present a clear text for the readers' interpretation and entertainment. This is especially so in the case of dialogue where what is said can suggest alternative interpretations. ❞

A reader will scan dialogue and look for subtext. In a scene where a wife is being questioned by a suspicious husband the wife could respond with the words:

'Darling, since we married you're the only man I've slept with.'

Within the confines of the story the character's husband could take this as a declaration that she is innocent of his accusations of infidelity. To the reader this could show:

- the character is lying – she's just come from her lover's bed;
- the character is being evasive – she's never *slept* with another man: she always stays awake;
- the character is being evasive – she has tactfully made no mention of the same-sex relationship in which she is currently involved.

EXERCISE

Using dialogue *only*, show a couple flirting. Don't use any physical descriptions or modifiers and concentrate solely on what they are saying to each other. Make extensive use of double entendre and try to make the exchange as realistic as possible.

Take the dialogue from the exercise above and add physical descriptions and speech tags/modifiers where necessary. Include appropriate mention of body language, facial expressions and any physical contact.

The reasoning behind these exercises is to show the writer the difference between creating dialogue that is 'all speech' and creating dialogue that carries non-verbal details of the character speaking those words. A single novel can contain examples of both types of dialogue so it is prudent for writers to master both styles.

Compare the texts you've created from these examples and see which you prefer. Judge the two pieces separately and try to decide which of them best conveys the essence of the scene you were trying to create. Make a careful note of what works well in one and what doesn't work as effectively in the other. Ask a friend/reader to consider the two pieces and see if their opinion matches yours.

General dialogue

'I think that diversion down memory lane was enough for one evening,' Philip said. 'Maybe Roger can coax some more humiliating anecdotes from me in ten years time when we see him again?'

Roger ignored Philip and leaned across the table. He took Annabel's hand in his, engulfing her tiny white fingers in his huge brown fist, and said, 'Philip was known as Assman by some of the folks on campus.'

'Assman?' Annabel echoed.

'No one ever called me Assman,' Philip interrupted.

'He had a thing for going in the back door,' Roger explained.

Annabel frowned as she tried to work out what this meant. When understanding finally washed over her, she couldn't decide whether she should be reacting with outrage or amusement. It didn't help that Roger's earnest expression inspired a wealth of unbidden urges. The light pressure of his hand around hers was a constant reminder of the attractive man's nearness. The lingering scent of his cologne continued to ignite her senses.

'Philip was into anal sex?' Annabel said carefully. She whispered the final words as though naming a shameful, dirty secret.

Leigh, A., Shared Wife

There's a three-way conversation going on in this scene between Philip, Roger and Annabel: hence the need for speech tags.

❦ In this scene we get a sense of Annabel's naivety contrasted against the worldliness of the two men sharing dinner with her. If the narrator of the story had told us that Annabel was comparatively innocent, the revelation would have been too expository – it would have been telling rather than showing. But, in this scene, the dialogue allows us to hear that Annabel is out of her depth.   ❧

When Annabel first repeats the word '*Assman*' it's obvious she has no idea why her husband had such a rude nickname. No doubt readers have already guessed why Philip had such a striking nickname, allowing them to savour the fact that they have more worldly knowledge than the naive Annabel.

- ◆ This does not mean that readers think Annabel is stupid.

- ◆ It doesn't even mean that readers think themselves to have superior knowledge.

Readers simply realise that Annabel is not worldly and they've discovered this through the subtext of the dialogue.

EXERCISE

Write a short three-way conversation. Your central characters are a couple enjoying an intimate dinner in a restaurant. A single school friend passes the table and recognises one of the couple.

How does the conversation go?

Be sure to include details such as speech tags, for clarity. Try to show whether or not the school friend's presence is appreciated or unwelcome.

Erotic dialogue

'So don't leave me just yet. Come to my house.'

I gently tugged my wrist free of his grasp. 'I can't go with you. I don't even know you.'

He studied me carefully as if memorising me. 'You know me. And you're afraid of what I know about you.'

Almost against my will, I asked, 'What do you know about me?'

His fingers took my wrist once more. 'I know you're nervous, a little afraid.' His grip tightened. 'I also know, if I asked you to go to the restroom and remove your panties, they would be soaking wet.'

I gasped, but I didn't attempt to pull away. Nor did I deny his statement. How could I? I'd been wet since I'd spotted him in the grocery store.

He smiled. 'Good. I didn't want another argument.' He rubbed his thumb over the pulse in my wrist. 'Now, do you want to come with me?'

Wright, K., 'In the Stacks'

❛ In erotic fiction flirting is one of the earliest aspects of intimacy and can be a prelude to intercourse. Presented unconvincingly, flirting can come across as flat, laughable and little more than an excuse to provide a bridge between sex scenes. Portrayed convincingly, flirting can present an exciting insight into the characters involved and can increase tension within an enjoyable erotic narrative. ❜

One of the most erotic aspects of an encounter between two characters is the flirting that takes place prior to physical intimacy. This is a frequently foregrounded feature of erotic fiction because this verbal foreplay allows the tension between two characters to slowly build.

- ◆ Flirting is a socially acceptable way of indicating sexual interest without suffering embarrassment.

- ◆ Flirting is a socially acceptable way of indicating sexual interest without causing offence.

- ◆ Flirting is rich in double entendre and innuendo so that the speaker's explicit intentions are veiled behind shades of potential meaning.

This means each speaker in a flirtatious conversation is in a position to apologise and say '*I didn't mean that*' or '*No! You misunderstood*' if their interest is rejected or perceived as inappropriate or unwanted.

EXERCISE

Write an erotic scene that takes place over a telephone conversation. It's a wrong number and the pair speaking decide to flirt. The point of view character has no way of knowing what the other character is doing. Use only dialogue to convey a growing sense of intimacy between these two separate characters.

Pillow talk

'What are your plans for the weekend?' she said. Actually, she lisped. The sound of her coy, little-girl voice grated on Edmond's ear, just as her toes rubbed clumsily against his cock. He felt himself stiffen.

'Uh, I'm going to . . .'

'Yes?' Sophie corkscrewed her big toe against his balls. Her big sky-blue eyes went round.

'The Botanics.'

'Tomorrow, right?' Sophie narrowed her eyes and licked her lips, her tongue flickering over the red lip-gloss. 'But tonight you're going to take me home and fuck me senseless.'

Magennis, N., 'Essence'

The conversation here is sexually explicit. Edmond is irritated by Sophie's little-girl voice but he makes no objection to her intimate touches and does not dismiss her offer of an evening's entertainment. At all times the dialogue in this story sounds like the credible exchange between a genuine, intimate couple.

❛ In all forms of creative writing credible dialogue is necessary. As previously stated, all fictional dialogue should suggest an accurate representation of a character's speech and be clearly understood by the reader. However, unless a writer has lived a very unconventional lifestyle, their first-hand knowledge of typical dialogue in an intimate erotic situation is likely to be limited. ❜

We get an idea of appropriate dialogue by listening to examples. However, this can be a problem for those writing erotica.

♦ If a writer wants to write a medical romance there is the opportunity to consult with doctors and nurses, or simply loiter around a hospital, to hear subject-specific conversations.

♦ If a writer wants to create a historical story there are period dramas that can be watched, as well as contextual dictionaries devoted to the words and language used for specific periods and situations.

♦ Yet, unless an author has some very open-minded acquaintances, there is little opportunity to experience first-hand examples of different characters speaking during their most intimate and erotic interludes.

It's worth remembering that, while this lack of opportunity for accurate research can be limiting in some regards, the vast majority of readers are in the same predicament. No one knows what happens in every bedroom. As authors, we can confidently write the words our characters will say in the situations where we've placed them.

The following pointers might be useful for structuring erotic dialogue so that it is at its most effective.

♦ Somewhere between flirting and fornicating, each character's speech should move from lengthy sentences to shorter ones.

♦ In passionate erotic scenes, characters often speak with a level of urgency that matches their physical state of excitement.

♦ The more intense a scene becomes, the more likely it is that characters simply grunt and use single syllable exchanges.

EXERCISE

Select any of the following scenes:

♦ Two platonic business colleagues discover they will have to share their hotel room at an out-of-town conference.

♦ An innocent card game between two couples turns into a game of strip poker.

♦ Two guests at a fancy dress party/masked ball converse without inhibitions.

♦ During a conversation between an established couple and one of their closest friends, someone says the word *threeway*.

Now, develop the conversation between the characters.

- What happens next?

- How does the scene develop?

Create dialogue that builds a scene and moves the characters towards an erotic encounter. Structure the erotic dialogue so that it matches the passionate involvement of the characters. Attempt to write 500 words on each of the practice exercises that you select.

SUMMARY

With dialogue the writer is trying to get the reader to read from the page what they usually hear with their ear.

- Keep all speech and related punctuation within speech marks.

- Everything else goes outside the speech marks.

- Use contractions.

- Use italics for stress and emphasis.

- Use speech tags for clarity.

- Only replicate accents when it's absolutely necessary.

Dialogue should always do one or more of the following:

- advance the plot;

- demonstrate character;

- show relationships;

- remain consistent for each character and always be specific to the situation and context.

Dialogue can be one of the most erotic ways for characters to interact.

- Have your characters flirt.

- Have your characters use innuendo and double entendre.

- Have your characters say things that only the reader will understand.

Dialogue is the part of our writing that readers always look for and that they most often remember when they have finished a story. Make full use of your dialogue.

8 Writing outside the box – form

It's easy to get fixated with one particular form or one particular type of content. Some readers I know have been reading novels for so long they can't remember the last time they read a poem. Some writers I know have been working in short fiction for so long they can't remember the last time they attempted poetry, novel-length fiction or non-fiction. As readers it will pay dividends to read outside our comfort zones. As writers, we can only benefit from dabbling with the unfamiliar.

WHAT I HAVE LEARNED ABOUT KISSING
That it's better approached gingerly, like a nervous mammal
That pheromones pass between us, suggestive of immortality
That crossing the streams does not end the universe
That breath can be swapped only so long before dizziness
That trumpet players' lips are more prone to dryness
That sometimes the mouth becomes all that exists
That breathing is less important than commitment to the kiss
That lip-reading means knowing a murmur's purpose
That the moment before connection should be prolonged
indefinitely
That the best kisses feel like both home and adventure
That teeth don't matter
That hands should be actively engaged
That eyes can be open but ought to be closed
That busy supermarkets spark memorable kisses
That kisses should occur whenever they are considered.
Vicky Ellis

Ellis's poem charts a heady list of associations with kisses. We read each line and we can compare Ellis's experiences with our personal recollections. The poem helps us remember our own kisses and the importance of them. Most importantly, it's a way of exploring the erotic outside the conventional forms of an erotic story, novella or novel.

EXPERIMENTING WITH OTHER FORMS

❝ Experimenting with other forms can help writers develop skills that are transferable across genres. Any writer who limits themselves to a single form of writing is missing out on a range of valuable opportunities. ❞

◆ Writing poetry forces a writer to develop a clear focus on the rhythm of words and phrases and the implication of each syllable.

◆ Writing flash fiction reminds the writer that every word counts.

◆ Writing flash fiction reminds the writer that quite a lot of words can be trimmed from a story.

◆ The single-minded focus of a well-written short story could be a powerful tool if it was used in a full-length novel.

◆ The overarching storyline from a series of related titles reminds us that sometimes the bigger picture is even bigger than was first imagined.

There are more variations in form than just poetry and fiction. Writers can make use of most writing styles and conventions.

◆ In *Fifty Shades of Grey*, Anastasia is confronted with legal documents contracting her submission to Christian Grey. These legal documents form a vital part of the story. The content of these documents, written in Christian's authoritative tone, is suggestive of Christian's control over Anastasia. It's also a striking and different way of presenting the story's content to the reader.

◆ In the same novel Anastasia occasionally communicates with Christian using emails. Emails and legal contracts are not typical devices for any form of fiction yet they work within the story being told by James. It would not be the same book without these devices.

◆ In 'The Sex Critic', a short story by Diane LeBow, the narrator takes the reader through a series of reviews of lovers: each one listed as though they were being appraised in a magazine either under a column for film reviews or art criticism. It's an unusual and unconventional approach to storytelling that makes the finished product all the more remarkable because it's so different.

Storytelling does not have to rely on the typical conventions of a narrator relating a story in chronological order. A story can be told in an infinite number of ways using an infinite number of forms. Experiment with the media and have fun with the various ways of presenting fiction to readers.

EXERCISE

Write down as many different forms as you can think of for getting words onto paper. Think about poems, songs, lists, reviews, articles, plays, essays, contracts, etc. Expand on this list and highlight those items that could possibly be used to bring some originality to a piece of fiction.

◆ Select one of these forms that's not normally associated with erotica (i.e. a list or an essay, etc.) and use it to start a piece that is erotic.

◆ Write a short erotic poem about kissing.

◆ Select one item from the list you've just created and incorporate it in an erotic scene.

Writing outside the box – content

9

Chastity: the most unnatural of the sexual perversions.

Aldous Huxley

If sex were simply a matter of inserting TAG A into SLOT B then there'd be little interest in erotica. However, because there are so many multifaceted approaches to sex, we have a genre that is rich in variation and deviation. Not even the most experienced writer will be familiar with every different aspect of sexual pleasure. Common aspects of contemporary erotica include:

- straight vanilla heterosexual;
- gay and lesbian;
- multiple partners;
- BDSM;
- kink.

The following pages do not claim to be exhaustive in listing sexual variety. They only provide an overview of some of the different ways that different characters enjoy pleasure.

Straight Vanilla

Lloyd sipped sagely at his red wine, his eyes narrowed, keen to pursue the conversational line.

'Well, without wanting to get too graphic at the dinner table . . .'

'Oh, no, I'm not talking body geography. I know the map of Sophie well enough, and I don't care how well-thumbed it is. I know where to plant my flag when I want her earth to move. I'm talking about places.'

'Places? Orgasmic places?'

'Yeah. Where's the strangest place you ever climaxed?'

'Oh . . . well. A swimming pool. An underground parking lot. A hotel balcony.' I frowned in an effort of memory.

'Tame stuff. Vanilla in the extreme. I'm surprised at you.'

'Lloyd! Where am I supposed to do it? Onstage?'

Elyot, J., 'The London O'

Vanilla heterosexual storylines are the commonest in erotica. Here we have the opening to a typical Justine Elyot story that promises to be far from vanilla, but the subject of that flavour is definitely on the table. Lloyd is clearly a man with a surprising sexual history to his credit if he can dismiss experiences in a swimming pool, an underground parking lot and on a hotel balcony as being 'vanilla'.

There are a lot of advantages to writing straight vanilla erotica:

◆ Straight vanilla erotica targets the largest audience.

◆ It's comparatively easy to find publishers for straight vanilla erotica.

◆ It's not difficult to research straight vanilla sex scenes because vanilla sex scenes are the mainstay of adult films and the most commonly discussed in contemporary literature.

> ❝ The identified taste of vanilla erotica can be altered by adding any of the flavours on the following pages and many more besides. However, it's worth remembering that many readers enjoy this flavour and don't want it changed. As writers we should focus on the stories we want to tell and the stories we believe our readers want to enjoy. ❞

Vanilla erotica is usually undervalued by critics. However, it's appreciated by writers and readers, which should really be the only concern for authors. Called *vanilla* because, like the ice cream flavour, it's virtually ubiquitous, vanilla erotica usually involves one heterosexual couple stretching no more boundaries than enjoying missionary position intercourse and maybe attempting oral sex.

EXERCISE

Write a vanilla sex scene. Your central characters have just had an enjoyable date. She's invited him in for 'coffee' and they've just shared a kiss. Write the vanilla sex scene that happens next. Aim for no more than 500 words.

GAY AND LESBIAN FICTION

I remember a couple of guys I had tricked with were there and I was drinking beer talking to them about their plant store when I first saw him. He was standing in a corner watching me. He wasn't smiling or glowering. He was just calmly watching me. I now know he must have been assessing me – wondering if he could bend my will and break me.

No. He wasn't wondering if he could do it; he was wondering if he wanted to do it. Mr. Benson never questions his own abilities.

Preston, J., *Mr. Benson*

Aristotle Benson in John Preston's novel *Mr. Benson,* is the archetype of the iconic leather-clad bad boy of gay fiction. The story, a boy-meets-boy romance with a sadomasochistic twist, is a well-written exploration of gay culture at the beginning of the 1980s. However, the gay culture and the sexuality are only a background to a compelling tale of one character falling reluctantly in love with another.

My girlfriend, Fennel, was still breathing hard when I worked up the courage to ask her a question. 'Why were you so rough that time?' I wondered aloud. I was glad we were in the dark so she couldn't see me blushing. I blush easily.

'Was I rough?' She playfully tweaked one of my nipples, pulling me closer.

'Well, not exactly rough,' I stammered. 'I mean, I'm not complaining, but . . .'

'Daisy,' she interrupted, 'you seemed to want it. So I gave it to you.'

My breath caught in my throat and I didn't trust myself to speak.
Roberta, J., 'Something Natural'

Jean Roberta's story 'Something Natural' is the tale of two characters deciding to add a new layer of kink to their existing relationship. Fennel and Daisy are sexually committed to each other and they want to explore new boundaries. The story follows their adventures as they discover the pleasures of spanking.

❝ Shortly after I'd written my first erotic novel, a reader approached me. Even though I'd published the book under a pseudonym she knew I was the author.

'I have to ask,' she began, 'how do you know what a lesbian thinks like?'

I can't remember how I answered. I do know I found the question puzzling. I hadn't consciously thought of the main character in my first novel as being lesbian: I'd only thought of her as a female character in a relationship with another woman. ❞

The identified sexuality of characters is only of consequence on two occasions:

◆ It's important if it's an essential part of the story.

◆ It's important if it's an essential part of the pitch to a publisher.

As Peter Tatchell, political campaigner and human rights activist, explains:

Who we are attracted to largely derives from a combination of social experience and ideology. In other words, everyone is born

with the potential to be queer. Exclusive heterosexuality is mainly the result of a socially-encouraged repression of same-sex desire.
Tatchell, P., *Beyond Equality*

It should be noted here that some erotica publishers deal exclusively with gay and lesbian fiction. Others deal only with heterosexual content. However, the majority are happy to consider material regardless of the identified sexuality of characters. Nevertheless, it's always worth checking a publisher's catalogue to find out if the content they publish matches the material you are producing.

EXERCISE

Read a book or short story from a contemporary gay or lesbian erotica catalogue. Select one that is intended for a readership outside your preferred sexuality. Explore how the erotica is written.

As a reader, is it possible to engage with the characters even when you don't identify with their sexuality? Does the erotica remain arousing even though it's not aimed at your sexual preferences?

MULTIPLE PARTNERS: WHO'S DOING WHAT TO WHOM?

Jacob wanted them both. Most of all, he wanted to shower them with affection – his sweet, generous woman and the impassioned, adoring friend who was so hungry for them. He ignored his erection long enough to stroke their heads, kiss their cheeks and their ears, and generally lend his blessing to the proceedings. Each of them kissed back at him, turning their heads to mouth and slobber at his face, kindly dolloping morsels of their arousal onto him, letting him participate in their liquid abandon. When Susan rattled in orgasm, her clenching cunt a flushed fussed-with mess in Normandie's hand, Jacob felt her teeth against his cheek.

Normandie's nipples, meanwhile, were dancing beneath Susan's fingers, and Jacob saw Normandie's entire body dance with

*them. Her hips, tight in jeans, sashayed on the cushions, and
Jacob knew that someone had better peel and fuck her at his or
her earliest convenience, before Normandie burned a hole
through the seat of her pretty pants.*

Edwards, J., *Rock My Socks Off*

Edwards shows a scene of wild and erotic abandon here. We
have two female friends, Susan and Normandie, enjoying an
intimate tryst with Jacob. However, although there are three
participants in this scene, Edwards makes sure the reader is in
no doubt about which character is being described when he
focuses on any particular aspect of eroticism. There are no
moments of doubt when we have to ask, 'Who's doing that?' or
'Which one is he talking about?'

6 One of the difficulties with any sex scene is that the reader can
be confused by what's going on and who's doing what. In a
straight vanilla liaison this problem is seldom noticed. When it's
only a man and woman involved the writer can say John, or
Jane, or *he* or *she*, or *him* or *her*, and the reader immediately
knows which character is being described. However, when there
are more than two people involved it becomes complicated as
the writer tries to quickly and unambiguously identify participants. There's a danger that a scene could become repetitive if
a character's name is repeatedly used. There's an equal danger
of confusion if the author simply says "she did this" or "he did
that".

Edwards gets round the problem of identifying characters by
repeatedly referencing Normandie by name. This approach feels
natural in this scene because the narrator character, Jacob, is in
love with Normandie. Under these circumstances it makes sense
for him to repeatedly use her name. However, another writer,
especially if they were addressing different character dynamics,
might take a different approach.

In scenes with multiple partners:

◆ Identify each participant before the intimacy begins.

◆ Make sure the reader knows what is going on.

- If there is any scope for confusion, address it fully.

- Pay close attention to these scenes during revisions and editing.

- Remember to use as much clarity as is needed.

EXERCISE

Write an erotic scene involving three people. It's the end of the evening after a successful party. An established couple are having a final drink with a friend that they both know and trust when someone brings up the subject of spanking. Write 500 words as this scene develops. Pay close attention to making sure there is no confusion as to who is doing what.

BDSM

'Good boy. Now drop them and sit here.' Her voice had taken on a much sterner tone. But even that didn't matter. Her instructions were exactly what he needed. His fingers opened, and his slacks slid down his legs and pooled around his ankles. He sat in the chair she'd indicated, and leaned down to slip out of his shoes. Leather, brown oxfords, the smell, the feel – his cock pulsed against his belly. He pushed his pants off, and put them on the chair beside him, crumpled, unnecessary.

When he sat up straight, she was there, inches from him, her hip level with his face. His breath came in ragged gasps. Could he touch her, the dress, feel its leather softness? His hand rose, reached but was slapped away.

'Naughty. Take off your socks.'

Mason, J., 'Those Boots'

❛ A lot has been written on the similarities between pain and pleasure. Experts will argue at length about whether BDSM refers to humiliation and embarrassment, domination and submission or the dynamics of power relationships. The essential thing to remember for any writer tackling this subject is that BDSM in fiction is whatever it means to the characters in the story. ❜

In the passage above Jude Mason's central character has a fetish for shoes. Fetishes like these are not a common theme in BDSM stories but the elements of domination and submission are staples.

- The dominating character here gives direct commands.

- She talks to the submissive character in condescending terms.

- She invades his personal space.

- She disciplines him with physical punishment.

❛ It's already been mentioned that non-consensual sex scenes are taboo in genre erotica. BDSM scenes can sometimes blur the line between what is consensual and what is non-consensual. Reluctant submissives, yielding beneath the demands of forceful dominants, can be perceived as being coerced into acting against their will. The guidance on this area is to make sure it's clear that a character is a willing participant in events, even if they're still not sure it's what they want.   ❜

BDSM can become a fascinating area of study and a thrilling device for erotic fiction. Subgenres of BDSM include punishment, humiliation, spanking, bondage and discipline. A writer needs to be familiar with elements of all of these to write convincingly in these areas. All that's been said before on the topic of research applies in this area.

The main thing to remember with BDSM is that the genre focuses on the interplay of power relationships between dominant and submissive characters.

- These are not gender-specific roles.

- Either men or women can be dominant.

- Either men or women can be submissive.

- The power dynamics of a BDSM relationship can apply between characters of the same sex or the opposite sex.

EXERCISE

One of the commonest scenarios in BDSM fiction used to be that of the boss and the secretary. Invariably this would involve a male boss telling his female secretary that she was naughty and needed a good spanking for having mishandled some important correspondence. The narrative would then rely on a power dynamic where the secretary tried to make amends by enduring her deserved punishment.

Start writing this scene in its conventional form but give the scene a twist. Reverse the roles of the characters. Try writing this with a female boss and a male secretary.

Try writing the story with a male boss and female secretary. Have her take control as she threatens him with union reprisals for his suggestions of disciplinary action.

Try writing this scene with a female secretary who wants to be punished. Her boss is unaware that she is submissive.

Remember to keep the focus of the story erotic.

Remember, even if your character is a reluctant submissive, their acquiescence should always be consensual.

WRITING ABOUT KINK AND FETISH

I used silver tongs to pick five ice cubes from the bucket. They clinked into the highball glass, each one making the crystal sing a slightly different note. It was a matter of degree, really. Kink was candy coating that made sex tastier. Fetish was bittersweet, dark chocolate, straight up, the kind that made your teeth shrink against the intensity of undiluted flavour.

Fetish was sex deconstructed. Removed from my body to my mind. The rites of worship worshipped. The fetish was for the details. Someone once said that God was in the details, but others said that it was the devil. A devil I knew intimately.

I went into the bathroom and turned on the cold tap. The edge of the claw-foot tub made an uncomfortable seat. I set the highball glass in the soap dish and dropped the thick terry robe to the white tiled floor.

Bradean, K., 'Chill'

It's said that kinky is using a feather: perverted is using the whole chicken. It's worth keeping this useless maxim in mind if you're consciously trying to write kink because, whether your characters are using a single feather or the whole chicken, there will be three typical responses:

- one reader will think it's innovative;
- another will think it's passé;
- a third will think it's obscene.

Bradean's story above is a remarkable example of kink/fetish. As the title suggests, and as this passage shows, the central character is aroused by the cold. I'm oversimplifying the content of the story here but, because we normally associate arousal with raised body temperature, the unusualness of this fetish makes for a memorable story.

> ❝ Allow your characters to indulge in kink whenever it feels natural. Don't simply write about conventional arousal. Give your characters quirks and show they have interests outside the normal spectrum of what is tried and expected. Follow Bradean's example and bring your erotica to life with an unusual and unexpected twist away from the conventional. ❞

Anyone who has ever written more than three sex scenes discovers that the most exciting acts of intimacy can quickly become repetitive, dull and somewhat predictable. The in/out, up/down of prolonged intercourse, while pleasurable in reality, does not make for the most absorbing literature.

Exploring kinks and fetishes can make this aspect of writing more interesting. The word fetish comes from the Portuguese word, *feitiço*: artificial, charm. The term is usually applied to a person's obsessive focus: a fetish for high heels, or a fetish for leather, etc. Kinks and fetishes come in all shapes and sizes. A recent online article concluded that the top ten fetishes included:

- voyeurism
- exhibitionism

- golden showers;

- leather;

- rubber;

- vinyl.

However, because most people are fairly secretive about their personal fetishes and kinks, it's difficult to put a lot of faith in any purportedly public surveys. It's safer to accept that any item that can be the focus for a person's obsessions will hold the attraction of a fetish for someone. As writers we can exploit this fully for the entertainment of our readers.

> ❝ A few years ago, while reviewing a book that had the word *Amour* in the title, I quipped that I had mistakenly read the word as 'armour'. In response to this remark in the review, I received correspondence from someone sharing their passion for chain-mail and breastplates. ❞

EXPLORING SUPERNATURAL AND PARANORMAL EROTICA

'Well, it is genetic, you know. The whole undead thing was just something old Van Helsing told Stoker when his wife left him for a certain Transylvanian count.' He licked her blood from his lips and gave her a wry smile. One of his hands was working its way between her legs, his fingers finding her clit.

She pushed it away. 'So what's with all this vampire hunting crap?'

'It's the family business. Besides, it makes me better at it and I'm very selective about who I slay. Do you really have any complaints?' His blue eyes glowed a little in the dark as he managed to slip his hand back between her legs. This time she let it stay. Twilight was about to get a lot more interesting.

Lundoff, C., 'Twilight'

Vampires have long been associated with erotica. Even before the characters in Bram Stoker's *Dracula* sexualised these mythical creatures, the myths on which vampires are based had always been invested in a relationship with the erotic. Possibly this is because there has always been something erotic about the exchange of bodily fluids and the intimate life-and-death dance that characterises the relationship between the vampire and the victim. But the relationship between the erotic and the supernatural also extends to werewolves. The condition of being a werewolf is passed on by inflicting scratch marks, similar to those inflicted by passionate lovers. Most of the characteristic activities enjoyed by werewolves, the passion and aggression, take place beneath a full moon. And, after a night of werewolf high jinks, most werewolves awaken naked and in a state of confusion reminiscent of someone having awoken from a drunken one-night stand.

> ❛ The erotic aspect of the supernatural is perennially popular, for obvious reasons. Stories about the supernatural allow readers to confront their fears through literature. Because the fear of sex and sexuality is an essential part of our repressed western culture these stories work for a readership that is aware of these fears. ❜

The traditional characters of supernatural or paranormal erotica include vampires, werewolves and ghosts. It's worth remembering that these stories can incorporate a strong horror aspect as well as erotic aspects, although the level of horror needs to be carefully balanced depending on the publisher. As general rules:

◆ Vampires can be used to represent sly sexual predators.

◆ Vampires can also be used to demonstrate promiscuity and hedonistic abandon:
  ◇ they operate at night and sleep through the day;
  ◇ they bite and suck their victims;
  ◇ they are (most usually) attractive and desirable.

◆ Werewolves can be used to show characters who behave irrationally on certain days of the month.

◆ Werewolves can show the consequences of promiscuity.

- Werewolves can be central to stories about domination and submission:
  - they are invariably aggressive as werewolves;
  - there is often a level of control exercised in werewolf stories, from cages through to collars.

- Ghosts can be used to show that some characters have influence even when they no longer have a presence.

Obviously there are more ways of using each of these standard supernatural character. And there are obviously more characters and types of characters than vampires, werewolves and ghosts. The most important thing, for anyone wanting to write supernatural or paranormal erotica, is to read examples of what's already been done in these subgenres.

EXERCISE

It's a full moon. Your central character is alone, house-sitting for a friend, in an unfamiliar location. The house is large and empty. Your central character is in bed with a laptop, trying to write a short story about the solitude. And then there's a knock on the bedroom door.

Write 500 words on this scene. Use any supernatural or natural phenomenon that you think is appropriate. Eroticise this scene as you think works best.

SUMMARY

- Experiment with form.
  - Read voraciously.
  - Write poems and prose.
  - Write articles and essays.
  - Include poems, articles and essays in your prose.

- Experiment with content.
  - Read and write straight vanilla erotica.
    - Keep in mind that straight vanilla remains one of the most popular areas of erotica.
  - Read and write gay and lesbian erotica.

▲ Explore fiction that deals with sexualities outside your normal area of preference.

◇ Write scenes that involve multiple partners.

▲ Pay attention to correctly identifying each participant in scenes with more than two characters.

◇ Write scenes of BDSM power play.

▲ Experiment with the power exchange involved in bondage, discipline, sadism and masochism.

◇ Write about kink and fetishes.

▲ Explore kinks to give variety to your writing.

▲ Explore kinks to find new ways of telling stories.

▲ Explore kinks to make your stories compelling.

Preparing your story for publication

10

Books aren't written – they're rewritten. Including your own. It is one of the hardest things to accept, especially after the seventh rewrite hasn't quite done it.

Michael Crichton

Before you send any work to a publisher your text needs to be polished to perfection. As authors we don't just write: we rewrite and we rewrite and we rewrite. There are several layers and levels of edit that need to be addressed and many of them need to be revisited with each rewrite. In the first instance a writer of erotica should ask the following three questions:

- ◆ Does the story make sense?
- ◆ Is the storty erotic?
- ◆ Does the story need the erotic scenes?

Does the story make sense?

Is there a logical development from the beginning to the end? Consider some of the notes in the chapters here on plot and character.

- ◆ Does it seem as if the central character's story has been told as fully as is needed?
- ◆ Does anything more need to be added?
- ◆ Does anything need to be taken away?

Is the story erotic?

If the writer's intention was to produce something erotic, hopefully it will be erotic. If it no longer strikes the writer as being erotic might the story be better suited for a different genre?

❝ If a story isn't erotic, that's not to suggest that the writer has gone wrong. I've heard authors of horror stories say that they started writing a piece thinking, 'Won't this be funny'!

The result, in a horror story, is rarely funny. Most times it's simply terrifying. That doesn't mean the author has gone wrong. It only means that their story is more fitting for a different genre than the one they originally intended. ❞

Does the story need the erotic scenes?

It's true that erotic stories need erotic scenes. But that doesn't mean a story needs to contain sex scenes simply for the sake of sex. As with all writing, if a scene doesn't need to be there, it should be cut from the text. This applies to erotic scenes if they're only there to titillate. Every scene in a story should be there to either show something about a character or develop the plot or make some point. An erotic scene should not simply be there because it's been a few pages since the main characters got naked.

EDITING YOUR STORY

There are many ways of revising and editing material but not all of them work for every writer. The essential thing to remember with any revision is to strive for clarity. As writers, we're aiming to produce the best work within our capabilities. This is particularly important in erotic fiction and sex scenes.

The slightest confusion or opportunity for misinterpretation can distract a reader long enough to distance them from the story. Once that connection has gone it can be difficult, and sometimes impossible, to get the reader back into the storyworld. The following editing suggestions will hopefully be of some use to help ensure a narrative remains engaging.

◆ **Read carefully through what has been written**

There is no substitute for a careful rereading. Read your manuscript one word at a time. If you can't find the time to read your work, do you really expect a publisher, an editor or a reader to find the time for it?

◆ **Read the work aloud**

There is a difference between the way the eye 'hears' a piece of work and the way the ear hears it. Pay attention to anything that doesn't sound right or is difficult to articulate. Watch out for accidental tongue twisters. Be warned that this is the most effective way of proofing any MS before submitting it to a publisher.

❛ Prior to submitting a MS to a publisher, it's sensible to perform a series of revisions, each time focusing on one particular aspect. The following list should be helpful as a checklist. ❜

◆ **Revise for narrative voice**

Is your story first person, third person or omniscient?

Is it consistently in that voice?

If not, have you shifted deliberately from one to the other, or is this shift something that needs addressing?

◆ **Revise for plot structure**

Is your story coherent, logical and chronological?

Are there any gaping plot holes?

Are there any parts of the plot that need a fuller construction?

◆ **Revise for character**

Are the characters consistently represented and fully rounded?

Will the reader be able to empathise with the characters' desires and ambitions?

◆ **Revise for dialogue**

Does each character speak in a distinctive voice?

Is the dialogue necessary to either show character or develop plot?

Is the dialogue presented properly on the page?

♦ **Revise for repeated words**

Make sure there is some elegant variation in references to characters, places and other elements in the story.

♦ **Revise for spelling and grammar**

Never rely on the spell checker of computer software. Too often these can be set on the spellings for other languages (US/UK/CAN, etc.). If you have any doubts about spelling, confirm the word with the aid of a reliable dictionary from your own language.

Be sure that each sentence is grammatically sound. Grammar mistakes are easy to overlook and make a writer look as though they don't know what they're doing. Pay close attention to the grammatical structure of every sentence and check any area where you have doubts.

Finally, have a trusted friend read through the material and listen to their criticism.

♦ Select a friend who won't be offended by your material simply because it's erotic.

♦ Select a friend who will give you constructive advice about what works and what doesn't work.

♦ Heed their advice whenever you think it's appropriate.

♦ Don't be afraid to discount critical advice if you think the critic has misunderstood your motives as an author.

Successful writing is seldom about writing: it's usually about rewriting. Discovering what works to please the author, and comparing this with how it pleases readers, is the key to successfully creating works that meet with critical approval and commercial success. Experimenting with different approaches, trying to judge impartially which is closer to the author's original vision of how a scene would transpire, and coaxing constructive critical feedback from readers will help any author to achieve their best results.

PUBLISH AND BE DAMNED

'I thought it was all obscene,' Rose muttered. She shivered with distaste as her eyes fixed on the cover. The glossy picture showed a pair of breasts, ripe and inviting, almost pressed against the lens of the camera. Across their ample swell, nearly indiscernible because of the clever black and white photography, lay a shaded line that could have been the bruise from a crop. If the picture was meant to illustrate some of the obscenities she had read in the text, Rose thought this was exactly what the mark was supposed to be. She threw the novel into the car's foot well and stamped on it angrily.

Ashton, L., Servants of the Cane

There are a broad range of publishers in contemporary erotica, each looking for fresh, well-written material from a broad range of writers. The rules for finding and approaching publishers are the same for erotica as they are for mainstream fiction. It's a three-part process that is fairly straightforward.

- Read what the publisher wants.

- Read what the publisher publishes.

- Write something that you want to write and the publisher wants to publish.

We'll examine each of these steps in greater detail on the following pages.

READ WHAT THE PUBLISHER WANTS

A publisher that concentrates exclusively on erotic novellas for the gay male will not consider a manuscript of lesbian poetry. This seems like an obvious statement but it's surprising how many publishers regularly receive submissions that are inappropriate for their imprint.

Check submission guidelines for the publishers you want to contact. Submission guidelines are easy to locate on the majority of sites for erotica publishers. Type the name of the publisher and the words 'submission guidelines' into a good search engine and the links will be provided. Read the guidelines carefully. Before going any further make sure the publisher you're pitching to is appropriate for the fiction you want to produce.

Consider the following questions:

◆ Is the publisher currently considering submissions?

Some publishers have periods where they don't consider submissions because of holidays and publishing schedules, etc. There is no point in sending material to a publisher who has expressly stated that they won't be considering it during that particular period.

◆ What form does the publisher deal with?
◇ Non-fiction? Fiction?
◇ Poetry, flash fiction, short stories, novellas, novels, epics?

It doesn't matter how good the writing might be, if the form falls outside the publisher's area of interest, it is unlikely to be accepted. Don't send non-fiction to publishers who deal only in fiction. Don't send a novel to a poetry publisher. There is no sense in sending a screenplay to a publisher who deals only in flash fiction. Consider what the guidelines say about the form the publisher wants and abide by those restrictions.

◆ What content does the publisher want?
◇ Straight, gay, lesbian?
◇ Contemporary, historical, paranormal?
◇ Romantic erotica, general erotica or hardcore BDSM?

Publishers, especially the ones who've been trading for a while, know what their readers expect. Established publishers of erotica know the sexual boundaries of their readers. Although a writer might think that their story is appropriate, if it strays outside the publisher's existing boundaries it's not appropriate for submission.

❝ Above all else: adhere to the publisher's guidelines.

Many erotica publishing houses will issue regular calls for submissions where they explain that they're looking for erotic stories targeted on a particular theme, written for a specific audience, and set at a certain length. The stories that successfully meet the needs of these calls for submissions are those where the authors have adhered to the publisher's guidelines. ❞

READ WHAT THE PUBLISHER PUBLISHES

Knowing that a publisher is listed as an erotica publisher is not enough. Authors need to sample the material of a publishing house before making a submission.

◆ What type of vocabulary does the publisher accept?

◆ How much description is given during explicit scenes?

◆ Is this a publishing house that produces erotic literature, genre erotica or something else?

Aside from being a helpful way of deciding whether or not a publisher might be a useful outlet for an author's writing, the idea of understanding what each erotica publisher publishes should be high on every writer's list of priorities.

❝ Keeping up to date with who is publishing what in the industry allows authors to be more informed about what is working for readers, and what areas are potentially being overlooked. It should also give authors an idea of where the stories they're currently developing could be first pitched for the best chance of success. ❞

WRITE SOMETHING THAT YOU WANT TO WRITE AND THE PUBLISHER WANTS TO PUBLISH

Having already considered what the publisher wants to publish, it's now up to the author to write the material.

This book has illustrated how many authors in this genre successfully produce erotic fiction and engaging sex scenes. If, as an author, you still want to write erotic fiction:

♦ Make use of these examples where you feel they're applicable.

♦ Disregard the examples that you don't feel would be appropriate for your fiction.

♦ Write the erotic stories you want to craft.

♦ Make sure your fiction reaches the appropriate audience.

FINAL WORDS

Erotic fiction is a powerful form of literature. While some stories can provide insights into the human condition and others can sway our opinions about religion and philosophies, erotica consistently shows us that, as humans, we're driven by arousal and we will always be driven by arousal.

Erotic poems have survived from the writings of ancient Greek and ancient Rome. There are erotic aspects to the Bible, Shakespeare and a host of other books and writers not normally associated with sex and sexuality. The idea that words written so long ago can still inspire arousal in readers is a remarkable concept. Writing, producing and publishing erotic fiction means that we can continue to be a part of this distinguished tradition.

Glossary

BDSM Abbreviation for *Bondage and Discipline, Sadism and Masochism.* It's sometimes argued that the middle letters also represent the words Domination and Submission. Regardless of what the abbreviation means, BDSM refers to relationships that depend on obvious demonstrations of power and authority.

Bondage The act of physically restricting a partner's movement, either through ropes, cable ties, chains or some other form of restraint.

Contemporary Stories set in the present day in modern, identifiable locations.

Dental dam A dental dam is a thin, square piece of latex or silicone placed over the labia during oral-vaginal sex.

Fan fiction Fiction that includes existing characters or settings from another author's work. **Note:** be aware that the publication of fan fiction can incur copyright implications.

Flash fiction (sometimes called *micro-fiction*) Short stories with a very restricted length. Depending on the publisher, flash fiction limits can be anywhere between 50 and 300 words.

Golden showers Sex acts involving urine.

Masochism/masochist Refers to the act of deriving pleasure from suffering and those who gain their pleasure from receiving pain.

MS Manuscript.

Paranormal Fiction that involves elements such as vampires, ghosts, werewolves or any other supernatural phenomena.

Sadism/sadist Refers to the act of deriving pleasure from inflicting suffering and pain on others and those who gain their pleasure from causing pain.

Straight Heterosexual.

Swinging/swapping Consensual sexual interplay between partners already in existing relationships.

Supernatural Fiction that involves elements such as vampires, ghosts, werewolves or any other paranormal phenomena.

Threesome/threeway Sexual relations between three people.

Vanilla Sexual pairings such as a man and a woman involved in the missionary position, usually derided for being unimaginative.

Bibliography

Anon, 1908, *Pleasure Bound: Afloat*, The Chatty Club, London.

Anon, 1909, *Pleasure Bound: Ashore*, The Chatty Club, London.

Arden, A., 2009, *The Girlflesh Captives*, Nexus, London.

Ashbless, J., 2012, *Named and Shamed*, Sweetmeats Press, London.

Ashton, L., 2001, *Servants of the Cane*, Chimera Publishing Ltd, Waterlooville.

Ashton, L., 2004, 'A Stout Length of Birch', *The Hot Spot*, Issue Number 2, p. 12.

Ashton, L., 2012, *Beyond Temptation*, Mischief Books, London.

Blue, C., 2008, 'The Hairy Matchmaker', in Green, S. and Valencia, R. (eds), 2008, *Lipstick on Her Collar*, Pretty Things Press.

Bradean, K., 2007, 'Chill', in Blue, V. (ed.), 2010, *Best of Best Women's Erotica 2*, Cleis Press, San Francisco.

Brown, T., 2008, 'Cling', in Bussel, R. K. (ed.), 2008, *Sex and Candy*, Pretty Things Press, San Francisco.

Bussel, R. K., 2011, 'Blow Me', in LaRousse, J. and Sade, S. (eds), 2011, *Nice Girls, Naughty Sex*, Seal Press, Berkeley, California.

Casanova, J., 1894, *The Memoirs of Casanova*, G. P. Putnam & Sons, London.

Clark, M., 2008, *Seduce Me*, Kensington Publishing Corp., New York.

Da Costa, P., 2006, *Entertaining Mr Stone*, Black Lace, London.

de Sade, Marquis, 1785, *120 Days of Sodom*, Solar Books.

de Sade, Marquis, 2004, *Juliette*, Olympia Press, London.

de Sade, Marquis, 2004, *Justine*, Olympia Press, London.

DooLittle, D., 2005, 'Clean Panties', in Dawn, A. and Kelly, T., 2005, *With a Rough Tongue*, Arsenal Pulp Press, Vancouver.

Du Pré, J., 2009, 'Before the Move', in Du Pré, J. (ed.), 2009, *Swing!*, Logical-Lust Publications, Hurlford.

Edwards, J., 2010, *Rock My Socks Off*, Xcite Books, London.

Ellis, M., 2006, *Dark Designs*, Black Lace, London.

Ellis, V., 2012, 'What I have Learned about Kissing', *No Sooner Knew the Reason but They Sought the Remedy*, weblog post, 23 August 2012, accessed 24 August 2012, http://deadgoodpoets.blogspot.co.uk/2012/08/no-sooner-knew-reason-but-they-sought.html.

Elyot, J., 2010, 'The London O', in Bussel, R. K., 2010, *Orgasmic*, Cleis Press, San Francisco.

Elyot, J., 2012, *Game*, Mischief, London.

Emerald, 2007, 'Who's on Top?', in Tyler, A. (ed.), 2007, *G is for Games*, Cleis Press, San Francisco.

Fox, A., 2011, 'Once You Go Black', in Riley, C. (ed.), 2011, *Too Much Boogie*, Logical-Lust Publications, Hurlford.

Germain, S., 2008, 'All About the Girls', in Bussel, R. K., 2008, *Tasting Her*, Cleis Press, San Francisco.

Grace, K. D., 2012, *Body Temperature and Rising*, Xcite Books Ltd, London.

Green, S., 2009, 'Pulling', in Green, S. and Valencia, R. (eds), *Lesbian Cowboys*, Cleis Press, San Francisco.

Grey, V., 2010, 'Shame Game', in Jakubowski, M. (ed.), 2010, *Sex in the City, London*, Xcite Books, London.

Hamilton, L., 2000, *Fire & Ice*, Black Lace, London.

Hartnett, A. M., 2012, 'Safe for Work', in Bussel, R. K., 2012, *Irresistible*, Cleis Press, San Francisco.

Houston, M., 2008, 'Tempted', in Tyler, A., *L is for Leather*, Cleis Press, San Francisco.

Jacob, A., 2008, *As She's Told*, Pink Flamingo Publications, Richland, MI.

James, E. L., 2012, *Fifty Shades of Grey*, Arrow Books, London.

Keck, K., 2005, *Oedipus Wrecked*, Cleis Press, San Francisco.

Kent, S., 2009, 'Aisle Seat', in Bussel, R. K., 2009 (ed.), *The Mile High Club*, Cleis Press, San Francisco.

King, D. L., 2011, 'The Treatment', in King, D. L., 2011, *Carnal Machines*, Cleis Press, San Francisco.

LeBow, D., 2004, 'The Sex Critic', in Szereto, M. (ed.), 2004, *Foreign Affairs*, Cleis Press, San Francisco.

Leigh, A., 2012, *Shared Wife*, OC Press, USA.

Levy, Caralee, 2005, 'Independence', in Green, S. and Valencia, R., 2005, *Rode Hard, Put Away Wet*, Suspect Thoughts Press, San Francisco.

Lister, A., 2009, 'The Twenty-Minute Rule', in Du Pré, J. (ed.), 2009, *Swing!*, Logical-Lust Publications, Hurlford.

Lloyd, K., 2012, 'All My Lovers in One Room', in James, T. (ed.), 2012, *Stretched*, Rubicund Publishing, Duluth.

Lundoff, C., 2007, 'Twilight', in Tan, C., 2007, *Best Fantastic Erotica*, Circlet Press Inc., Cambridge, MA.

Madden, M., 2007, 'Under Her Skin', in Lloyd, Da Costa and Madden, 2007, *Lust Bites*, Black Lace, London.

Magennis, N., 2007, 'Essence', in Tyler, A. (ed.), 2007, *E is for Exotic*, Cleis Press, San Francisco.

Magennis, N., 2010, 'The Red Shoes (Redux)', in Tyler, A. (ed.), 2010, *Alison's Wonderland*, Spice Books, Ontario.

Marsden, S., 2009, 'The Student', in King, D. L. (ed.), 2009, *The Sweetest Kiss*, Cleis Press, San Francisco.

Martin, D., *Twilight Girl*, Cleis Press, San Francisco.

Mason, J., 2008, 'Those Boots', in Tyler, A., 2008, *L is for Leather*, Cleis Press, San Francisco.
Masters, G., 2007, 'Better than Brazil', in Roux, J., 2007, *Erotic Tales 2*, Erotictales Publications.
Miller, Rev. J., 2009, *Live Nude Elf*, Soft Skull Press, Brooklyn.
Moore, M., 2009, *Sarah's Education*, Black Lace, London.
Morizawa, J., 2010, *Memoirs of a Wannabe Sex Addict*, Fanny Press, Seattle.
Perks, M., 2008, 'The Performing Breasts', in Fixter, A. and Dubberley, E. (eds), 2008, *Ultimate Burlesque*, Xcite Books, Treharris.
Perks, M. and Mullins, K., 2006, 'Underneath', in Szereto, M. (ed.), 2006, *Dying for It*, Thunder's Mouth Press, New York.
Pita, M. I., 2007, *Safe Words & Spells*, Magic Carpet Books Inc., New Milford.
Portnoy, S., 2006, *The Butcher, The Baker, The Candlestick Maker*, Virgin Publishing Ltd, London.
Preston, J., 1983, *Mr. Benson*, Cleis Press, San Francisco.
Quinn, D., 2007, *Flesh and the Devil*, Aphrodisia Erotic Romance, New York.
Réage, P., 1970, *Story of O*, The Olympia Press, London.
Remittance Girl, 2009, 'Midnight at Sheremetyevo', in King, D. L. (ed.), 2009, *The Sweetest Kiss*, Cleis Press, San Francisco.
Riley, C., 2011, 'It's Tight Like That', in Riley, C., 2011, *Too Much Boogie*, Logical-Lust Publications, Hurlford.
Roberta, J., 2008, 'Something Natural', in Forbes, M., 2008, *Seriously Sexy 1*, Xcite Books, Treharris.
Sacher-Masoch, L., 1870, 'Venus in Furs', in *Legacy of Cain, Volume 1*, J. G. Cotta Verlag, Stuttgart.
Sarai, L., 2004, 'A Quiet Evening at Home', in Kramer-Bussel, R. (ed.), 2004, *Naughty Spanking Stories from A to Z*, Pretty Things Press, San Francisco.
Scott, E., 2007, *Naughty Housewives*, NAL Heat, New York.
Starr, D., 2004, *Designed for Sin*, X Libris, London.
Storey, D. G., 2007, *Amorous Woman*, Neon, London.
Szereto, M., 2009, 'Rapunzel', in Szereto, M., 2009, *In Sleeping Beauty's Bed*, Cleis Press, San Francisco.
Tyler, A., 2009, 'Some Like it Hot', in Tyler, A. (ed.), 2009, *Playing with Fire*, Cleis Press, San Francisco.
Walker, S., 2007, 'Counting the Days', in Kramer-Bussel, R. and Tyler, A. (eds), 2007, *Hide and Seek*, Cleis Press, San Francisco.
Walker, S., 2008, 'TGIF', in Tyler, A. (ed.), 2008, *Open for Business*, Cleis Press, San Francisco.
Wright, K., 2004, 'In the Stacks', in Morley, N. T. (ed.), 2004, *Master/Slave*, NAL Heat, New York.

Index